# WRESTLING PRAYER

## ERIC & LESLIE
## LUDY

HARVEST HOUSE PUBLISHERS

EUGENE, OREGON

Eric and Leslie Ludy: Published in association with Loyal Arts Literary Agency, LoyalArts.com.

*Cover by Abris, Veneta, Oregon*

*Cover photo © Stockbyte Photography / Veer*

**WRESTLING PRAYER**
Copyright © 2009 by Winston and Brooks, Inc.
Published by Harvest House Publishers
Eugene, Oregon 97402
www.harvesthousepublishers.com

Library of Congress Cataloging-in-Publication Data
Ludy, Eric.
Wrestling prayer / Eric and Leslie Ludy.
   p. cm.
ISBN 978–0-7369–2165–7 (pbk.)
1. Prayer—Christianity. 2. Spiritual life—Christianity. I. Ludy, Leslie. II. Title.
BV210.3.L835 2009
248.3'2—dc22

2008054856

# Contents

# TOSSING THE GIRLISH SENSIBILITIES

❧ LESLIE ❧

I'm a girly girl. I oooh and ahhh over a bouquet of beautiful flowers, I squeal and run at the nearby buzz of a bumblebee, and I love being held close in the arms of my man.

Simply put, there's nothing innately inside me that wants to wrangle with a bear, ride a mechanical bull, or crawl in the mud. I prefer things neat, tidy, and smelling sweet.

While Eric loves the idea of "wrestling," it is not something I'm naturally inclined to gravitate toward. It's always mystified me why guys like to roll around on the ground interlocked, sharing sweat, and miserably contorted. The whole notion of wrestling is very unfeminine. It's a smelly, sweaty, bloody business, and if it weren't for the Spirit of God, I might never have come near it.

There is absolutely nothing wrong with being girly. Nothing, that is, unless it stands in the way of God bringing about the fullness of His gospel life within us.

A study of Scripture reveals that our God is a wrestler. He's a fighter. He's a manly, valiant, mighty warrior. And the business of His kingdom is often smelly, sweaty, and bloody. His mighty men have been splattered with the blood of battle, His prophets have died grisly deaths, His messengers have been beheaded, sawn in two, and impaled in the most horrific fashion.

There is nothing girly about Jesus picking up a whip and strolling into the temple to purge it of crooked merchants. And the idea of Jesus sweating great drops of blood, being scourged with a cat-o'-nine-tails, and being unceremoniously nailed to a bloody cross makes me squeamish.

God made me a girl. And He did that on purpose. But He asks me to become the kind of girl who is actually useful to His kingdom purposes. I need to become the sort of girl who is unafraid to poke my head into the battle of the ages and cry out, "Who is this uncircumcised Philistine who is blaspheming the armies of the living God?"

God wants me to wrestle. God wants to stick grit in my girliness. He wants me to be prepared to tangle, to interlock my soul in this eternal combat—not with other girls, not with sweaty boys, but with Him, and with the otherworldly powers of darkness. He wants me to wrestle in prayer, to grab ahold of His great and precious promises and fight to see them unfurled in living reality on this Earth.

What you are about to read is a book more easily grasped by the mudslinging, spit-wad shooting, crawdad collecting sort of audience that has an inherent well of testosterone to draw from. But this isn't a book just for men, any more than the Bible is.

Christianity has confused catching mice with the real work of the kingdom, which is more like hunting lions. We've lost the sacred work of prayer. And we no longer know how to wield the power of God in this world. Lions, bears, and blaspheming giants are having their way in the church today, and it is high time that we start doing something about this travesty.

No, I have not lost my girlishness. However, I can say I have become a huge fan of wrestling...at least God's version of it. I still get a bit squeamish around smells, sweat, and blood, but God is toughening me in all the right ways. This girl is learning how to deal out a mean uppercut to the enemy's smirking jaw—and, I must admit, it's quite satisfying to see him whimper in pain.

I personally know no other man who can speak on the issues this book presents better than my husband, Eric. This book is merely a peek into his life—this stuff is his daily diet. He's a man acquainted with both the prayer closet and the public arena of proclamation. Eric is a wrestler. He understands the power of prayer and he wields it mightily. The truths in this book aren't merely ideas he thinks about; they are principles he lives each day. So Eric is going to lead us in this grand and epic conversation. Then, at the end of each chapter, I'll add my two cents of practical application and real-life analogy.

This isn't just another book about the disappointments and disillusionments of unanswered prayer. And even though there are many practical truths woven in these pages, this is not primarily a prayer how-to book. Rather, it's a soul-stirring message about the explosive possibilities of true wrestling prayer. This message may seem larger-than-life at first. But I believe that if you take this book to heart, your spiritual life will never be the same. In fact, history will never be the same!

An important note: In this book, we have chosen to use a lot of Old Testament stories to illustrate God's intentions for our Christian lives today. "Aren't those just stories?" some might question. "The historical accounts in the Old Testament can't possibly be a prescription for us in our New Testament Christian life, can they?" Yes, they are stories, but Eric and I believe they are stories purposely crafted by God to hold great meaning and depth for our lives today. They are stories with layers of God-intelligence packaged in them. He sovereignly directed the formation of these stories and included them in His Word for a very specific purpose: to help us not only recognize Christ, but learn how to live out the life of Christ. As the apostle Paul says of all Scripture, including the Old Testament, it's all "profitable for teaching" (2 Timothy 3:16). In other words, it's useful for the practical real world Christian life of following Christ, knowing Christ, and revealing Christ to this world.

In the New Testament, whenever there is a specific prescription for the Christian life (that is, be holy, believe, be pure, offer thanks, walk in the Spirit and not in the flesh), the Old Testament can be utilized to help interpret what the New Testament is saying.

In the Old Testament, God's people fought external, physical battles for His glory. Because of Christ's work on the cross, the battles we fight are now primarily internal, spiritual battles for His glory. Where once the temple of God was a building made of stone, now our very bodies have become His temple—housing the very presence and Spirit of God. We are called to fight for His honor and glory in our own lives, just as the people of the Old Testament were called to fight for His honor and glory in their physical battles. And the Old Testament exploits of God's warriors provide an excellent picture of the adventures we face each day in the spiritual realm.

This message may seem larger-than-life at first. As you read, you may think, *But I'm just a college student, or a store clerk, or a stay-at-home mom. How can these epic truths apply to my life?* Well, just so you know, Eric and I aren't extraordinary people either. We have never wrestled lions and bears or gone marching into battle against the Philistines. But in the process of exploring the amazing patterns and principles from God's Word that we discuss in this book, our boring lives have truly become a grand adventure.

Dr. Goulburn, Dean of Norwich, once said, "The greatest Old or New Testament saints were on a level that is quite within our grasp. The same power that was available to them is also available to us." That statement is the message of this book. For Eric and me, it's the essence of how God has called us to live, and it's the message He's called us to proclaim to others.

As Eric and I have taken that statement to heart, our lives have been completely and utterly transformed. And no matter who you are or how ordinary your life seems, we believe that if you approach this book with a heart fully yielded to Christ's Spirit, your spiritual life will never be the same. In fact, history will never be the same!

This dying world needs more men and women who are ready and willing for a spiritual tangle. I hope and pray that you will be among the first to answer the sacred call.

PS: There are a couple crucial elements of prayer, namely, fasting and intercession, that Eric and I chose not to tackle in this book. We see these as "next phase" areas of prayer that can more effectively be explored after the principles discussed in these pages are already at work in a believer's life. To truly do justice to the grand and epic dimensions of both fasting and intercession, we would need to write a whole separate book—which, Lord willing, we might do in the near future. In the meantime, if you are interested in these topics, a good starting place would be the other books on prayer that we've recommended in the following pages.

# A Generation of Legendary Heroes
*discovering the epic adventure*

❧ Eric ❧

My brother, Mark, just opened up the coolest coffee shop here in Windsor, Colorado. I'm not much of a coffee guy, but I do have an affinity for a classy coffee shop—the aromas, the people, the ambiance.

The routine so far is as follows: I order myself a skinny 16-ounce decaffeinated iced chai tea and claim for myself a small table in the cozy enclave behind the fireplace. With a little arm-twisting from my brother I did try a Thai tea the other day, and I did give the spiced hot chocolate a whirl last Wednesday—both were superb. However, I really like my chai tea—I have a propensity to find my ruts and bask in their predictability.

As of this morning, Loodles Coffee, Books, and Art has been open 14 days. So here's the problem: During those 14 days I have logged 23 visits. In other words, I really like this place. And my concern is, this place just might be too comfy of an environment in which to write a book on such a grand (and forgive me, girls), hairy-chested theme as this manuscript boasts. It's almost like writing about Shackelton's great adventure to cross Antarctica while sipping a pina colada on the beaches of San Martin.

Now, to be fair, it might prove difficult to find the correct habitat in which to write this book if it needs to perfectly match the gritty content contained herein. For instance, I probably should be dangling from the side of a Moabian cliff crammed into a small tent, or possibly running with the bulls along the cobbled streets of Pamplona. But the idea of writing this book while hanging from a cliff or being chased by an angry bull leads me to one very problematic issue—where would I plug in my laptop?

This is a book for the hungry—it's for men and women of God who are ready to see things changed in the modern church, believers who ache over the loss of true living spirituality and are ready to do whatever it takes to get it back.

Windsor, Colorado, may not seem like the ideal location in which to write this book. After all, where is the danger in Windsor? Where are the angry bulls? Isn't Windsor just a little Norman Rockwell village in the heart of comfortable, self-absorbed America?

Yes, on the outside Windsor may appear a bit soft, but God is doing something right here in Windsor—something big, something gritty, something mighty. God is taking mousy men and women and transforming them into heroic champions of truth.

Now I realize that with my recent confession of 23 visits to Loodles in the past two weeks it would definitely seem as if I too am living the pampered life of sugary mochas and flavored lattes. However, during most of those 23 visits I was accompanied by a desperate young man in the throes of spiritual battle.

Loodles has become my Cave of Adullam (see 1 Samuel 22:1). It's my Arthurian Round Table, my general's tent. Over the past two weeks this coffee shop has entertained some of the most vigorous spiritual conversations, some of the most life-altering dialogues, as well as some of the most hallowed discussions on the sacred themes soon to be unfolded within this book.

I sat in Loodles just yesterday, across the table from a 28-year-old man named John, and I saw the fire of the Almighty blaze within his eyes. I saw him awaken to the vision of a heroic growling prayer life, I watched him respond to the call, and I listened to him plead with his heavenly King for a place among His most mighty and most valiant men.

Early last Saturday morning, I witnessed a young man named

Jeremy come strolling in for breakfast after spending nearly seven straight hours in wrestling prayer—his eyes full of fire, his gait marked by the confident stride of the freshly anointed.

Just this past Friday, it was a young buck named Bobby who stared me square in the eyes and said, "I've found it!" He had the treasure of God in his possession; he was holding in his spiritual grasp the blazing fire of the Spirit; and let me tell you, it was a sight to behold.

A week ago Thursday, it was a 23-year-old warrior-poet named Matt. A week ago, Wednesday, it was a modern-day Martin Luther named Ben. The list could go on and on. And that doesn't even include all the valiant young women whom Leslie has interacted with. The battle is fierce, and these men and women are on the front lines. And, as strange as it might seem, the gathering place for these grand and gritty discussions is (ahem) a coffee shop with a rather cartoonish name strangely akin to my own.

So here's our plan.

Leslie and I have decided not to write this book while hanging from the side of a cliff or being gorged by an angry bull. We've decided that we will write it right here at Loodles, in between all the grand and glorious conversations swirling around us. But please note: A conversation held here in Loodles isn't meant to stay in Loodles. It's meant to pick us up by the keister and throw us into the raging battle of souls—it's meant to move us to Uganda, Cambodia, East Timor, or even Brazil, to the darkest places on Earth to wrestle with the powers of darkness to see the little boy soldiers, the battered orphans, the hunted street children, and the five-year-old slave-prostitutes set free. I must forewarn you: A Loodles coffee shop conversation is far more dangerous than it actually sounds.

Dear reader, Leslie and I want you to feel the thrill of a gumption-packed conversation here at Loodles. It's like pure adrenaline injected into the bloodstream, molten steel applied to the spine, and the lionesque growl of the Spirit of God emanating from the human soul. Every believer must taste it to remind himself that he is still alive and there is a God who still sits firmly on the throne.

Leslie and I want you to join us. We don't want this to be a mere book, but a conversation—an epic, soul-stirring conversation between you and the two of us. If you are one of those characters who prefers a more formal invitation, then here it goes:

"Would you mind meeting up at Loodles in a couple minutes for some serious spiritual banter? We're buying!"

We've got our favorite table reserved by the fire while my skinny, 16-ounce iced chai and Leslie's 12-ounce piping hot peppermint tea are just waiting to be enjoyed. While you sip at your sugary mocha, we would like to share with you the vision God has for your life as a believer. We promise there will be moments of serious discomfort, moments when you will glance up at the exit sign and ponder running for the door. But if you hang in there with us, we promise, you will find more than just a new growl and gumption in your spiritual existence—you will find one of the most thrilling pictures of what your life on planet Earth can become.

If you are game, let's do it. And let's do it now.

While you are making your way over here to Loodles, let me give you a little more background that might prove important for our upcoming conversation. In the book world this is called an *introduction*, but in the coffee-shop-conversation-world it's kind of like looking at the menu.

I like to add a little bit of mystery to the books I write, but with a title like *Wrestling Prayer*, the cat's sort of already out of the bag as to what this book is about. It's about prayer, yes. But, the sort of prayer this book is about is nearly unheard of in our modern churches. And I can assure you, the way in which Leslie and I will address this topic will probably not be as you might expect.

This is a fun book. It's a book loaded with big thinking, big living, and big believing. It's a book that flows directly out of the most significant spiritual growth season of our lives. This book lets you into our prayer closet, where you will hear all the growing pains and all the hoots of victory—you will hear the sighs, the wonder, and the weeping right along with the jubilance of two people walking and leaping and praising God in a real-life land flowing with milk and honey.

This book isn't tame—it's death-defying. It's the stuff that builds happy martyrs and heaven-minded mighty men and women.

And it all flows out of an experiment.

Leslie and I launched this experiment two years ago. It has forever altered our lives, and God's pile driver of grace has driven home the substance of this book into our souls.

I'm hesitant to call it an experiment, because the word *experiment* denotes the idea of uncertainty. And there hasn't been uncertainty, per se, in our experiment, any more than there is uncertainty in touching fire to dynamite. We knew what would happen. But we just didn't know how big the explosion would be.

Leslie and I covenanted with our heavenly King to dedicate ourselves to prayer in a manner far beyond that which we had ever done before in our lives. We said, "What will happen if we make prayer our daily job description? What would happen if we spent the same energy on praying as we do on our marriage, our family, and our ministry?"

You see, two years ago we were knocked off our proverbial spiritual feet. We found ourselves on our backsides with those cartoonish little birdies tweeting around our dizzied heads. We had been hit, and hit *hard,* by the enemy. At that time, we had been on the front lines of Christian ministry for nearly 12 years—so we knew intimately how the spiritual fur can fly when the gospel is in the ascendant. But through all our many spiritual battles, we had always come through intact. But this incident was different. It was that feeling in the pit of the stomach that comes when one realizes that, while he was asleep, a thief had entered his house and made off with all his best stuff. It was a sense of extreme violation.

As the story goes, Leslie was pregnant and then suddenly one day she wasn't. She had miscarried. Somehow our precious little child had been violently touched. And the sorrow was tremendous. The Thief had come, and he had stolen, killed, and destroyed.

For most of my Christian life, whenever the enemy had attacked me with darkness and confusion, I'd simply assumed that God was causing or allowing it. But in grappling with this situation, through much prayer and intensive study of God's Word, Leslie and I began to realize that this attack had not come from Him, but from the enemy of our souls. God gently opened our eyes to see areas of sin and compromise that we'd allowed into our lives that were opening an access point for the enemy to hit us. As we repented of these things, we recognized for the first time that God did not want us to simply resign ourselves to the enemy's attacks. Rather, He wanted us to put on the full armor of God—to seal up every breach that would allow the enemy to gain access into our lives. And He wanted us to call upon His name and allow Him to come to our rescue in time of need. James 4:7 says, "Resist the devil and He will flee from you." Leslie and I hadn't been resisting the enemy's blows because we had assumed they were coming from God—or at least being *allowed* by God for the purpose of discipline. And yet, when we really thought about it, we had to admit that the result in our spiritual lives wasn't the life-giving victory that God's loving discipline brings. Rather, it was the hopeless despair and discouragement that the enemy brings.

I had always thought the most God-pleasing thing I could do when bad things happened was to simply accept them and move on. But God was showing me that when the enemy attacked, He didn't want me to accept it. Yes, the Christian life meant yielding to my Lord, even in difficult circumstances, and even when it caused pain and sacrifice. But it also meant standing up and fighting (in the power of His Spirit) against the enemy's intentions for my life. I'd never really been taught how to discern what I should yield to and what I should fight. But now, God was beginning to open my eyes to see it clearly.[1]

For better or worse, I've always been sort of an easygoing guy—a lover, never a fighter. But through this situation, something was awakened and kindled inside me. I'm embarrassed to say this, but in hindsight, I realize I was like one of those tame circus bears, groomed his entire life on steak dinners and dressed in a pink tutu for his circus act. And yet suddenly I was thrown into the Alaskan wilds, forced to hunt for fish with nothing but my furry paw, sleeping outside in the wind, rain, sleet, and snow, and desperately needing to discover my bear growl before I died of exposure to the elements. This is exactly what happened. And it seemed that just in time, I threw off that pink tutu, forsook my steak dinners, and started hunting like a brown bear is supposed to hunt.

Through all the miscarriage drama, my soul started rumbling with a growl, a fight, a heavenly snarl that I never even knew existed. It was as if Eric Ludy stood up to the enemy for the first time and said, "That's it! There will be no more of that! Do you hear me? I stand in the authority inherent in the mighty Name of Jesus and I say, 'Get out of here!'"

It took 36 years for God to get sweet, kind, sensitive, gentlemanly Eric Ludy to start growling like a lion and swatting fish like a bear. I'm horrified with how long I wore that crazy pink tutu. I pranced around unwittingly with a postmodernesque pansy gloss to my spirituality and I just couldn't figure out why it was so impotent and powerless to change this world. And then suddenly I was exposed to the harsh realities of the Alaskan wilds and I realized that my cozy little existence and my Home Depot-bought spiritual power tools wouldn't work out here where the air is frigid, the wild animals are not separated from me with a ten-foot ditch and a pane of Plexiglas, and where the nearest suburban electrical outlet was 200 miles away. I needed something that worked; something that got real results.

"God!" Leslie and I cried. "What must we do? What can we do?"

"Pray!" was the soft yet firm response from our King.

"We do pray!" we answered.

"That's not prayer," God seemed to say, "that's spiritual-sounding chitter chatter."

Leslie and I built our entire ministry upon the notion, the idea of prayer. And suddenly, two years ago, we began to realize that our ministry had been built on "spiritual-sounding chitter chatter." God's concept of prayer was something wholly different, something so much more majestic, epic, and grand—something Leslie and I knew very little about. But it was something that worked where the air is frigid, the carnivorous critters run wild, and where all other American-made plastic spiritual weaponry has no place to plug in.

Our personal version of prayer had always been very tepid, very pleasant, very sweet—the equivalent of a giggling little girl flitting about a living room dusting off the bookshelves with a feather duster. Ours were a maintenance sort of prayer, a house-cleaning kind of prayer. But God's concept of prayer is far more like picking up Ulysses's massive sword and swinging it with all the fire and ferocity of a desperately crazed warrior. God's version of prayer takes territory. It doesn't sit at home and clip spiritual coupons; it heads off into enemy territory to fight. Samson picked up the jawbone of a donkey and single-handedly slew a thousand Philistines, and we are supposed to pick up the jawbone of prayer and wreak untold spiritual havoc upon the enemy camp.

I'm guessing there are a few of you out there who don't particularly care for my "spiritual-sounding chitter chatter" comment. And that's probably due to the fact that you've been a spiritual chatterer your entire life and it ruffles your feathers a bit to think that you haven't really been engaged in holy, heavenly prayer.

It's not to say there has been no genuine spiritual engagement in our lives, for it's very likely there has been. But just like the Israelites in the wilderness had genuine experiences with God (a cloud by day, a pillar of fire by night, daily manna from heaven, and their shoes not wearing out for 40 years), they still were falling short of the life, the power, and the grandeur of living that God had called them to.

So, please bear with me as I poke at all of us chatterers a little more.

Spiritual-sounding chitter chatter tends to be self-centric in its banter, begging for comforts to be protected, deadlines to be met, surgeon's hands to be guided, tests to be passed, and food to be blessed. It's always about us. And, whereas there is nothing wrong with praying about our own personal needs, prayer—real-life historic prayer—is otherworldly and built upon the notion of a *forgotten* self. It's aggressive, growling, attacking, commanding, persevering, passionate, and feverishly unrelenting—it's battlefield firing, as if every utterance is chipping away at enemy strongholds and every petition is moving God's indomitable purposes forward in this natural realm.

Bona fide, heaven-inspired prayer—the kind that moves mountains and calms storms—is not something the modern church is used to. To be quite frank, it's not something Leslie and I were accustomed to either. And as a result, we (the modern church) often, with a dismissive wave of our hand, pass off this sort of wild-eyed praying as being "Old Testament" or "first century." Few of us have ever seen such prayer power in our generation, and therefore, we surmise that such prayer power no longer exists.

But study the lives of John Hyde, Rees Howells, David Brainerd, George Muller, Andrew Murray, E.M. Bounds, William Booth, and Leonard Ravenhill (to name a few), and you suddenly realize there is so much more to be found—prayer is nuclear in its power and revolutionary in its effect.

I remember reading stories about John Hyde (also known as Praying Hyde). This man would spend days, even weeks at a time on his knees in prayer and intercession. He would weep, he would laugh, he would sing, he would be laid flat before the awesome Holy Presence— he would shout, he would whisper, he would wrestle, he would fight until the victory was achieved.

John Hyde died of a heart condition—his heart literally moved from one side of his chest cavity to the other due to a near-constant strain and physical taxation upon it. It was the strain of prayer, the burden of the lost that he carried. And he knew full and well that it was killing him, but he considered it the highest honor to participate with his Christ in the office of an intercessor and thus to watch with his Lord in Gethsemane.

Those who know me know my reticence to being lumped in among the more questionable fringe elements in Christendom. However, even at risk of sounding like I've thrown out my scruples for a little gospel magic-show routine, I'm going to say it like I see it:

The power of God has not in the least bit been diminished over the past 2000 years. Our Lord still sits on His great throne and His train still fills the temple. He still walks on the wings of the wind, He still rides on the backs of the mighty cherubim, and He still is the Triumphant Champion from Calvary. All hell still bends to His will, and sin and death have lost their hold on all who rest in the shadow of His presence. And the God who calmed storms, raised up dead men to life, and multiplied fishes and loaves to feed thousands is the same God we have today.

And this is what Leslie and I believe with every fiber of our being. And we have believed this throughout our entire 15 years of ministry. But the two of us were missing something very important (for most of those 15 years) that takes this vast and epic reality and brings it home in our day and age—*the unrelenting givenness to wrestling prayer.*

Leslie and I haven't understood the purpose of prayer, the power of prayer, and the position of prayer, let alone the reality of what prayer does when engaged in according to God's design.

But two years ago, we began the "experiment" and, in doing so, have touched fire to dynamite. And as a result, there has been an explosion of spiritual growth within our lives.

Prayer in our modern day has been diminished and, as a direct result, the power of the church of Jesus Christ has seemingly vanished. We are not a triumphant lot anymore, but rather, a weak, sin-stained, defeated one. We've lost our strength, our confidence, our absolute assurance that our God is with us in battle. So many amongst our ranks are literally scared to fight because they honestly don't know if they are going to win if they do.

We've ventured a long way from our historic roots, and it's high time that we returned.

Unfortunately, books have limitations. As authors, Leslie and I long for this book to pin you down on God's operating table, inject you with whatever anesthesia is necessary to keep your arms from flailing about, and then do heart-transplant surgery on you—taking out your mousy heart and planting a lion's roar within your chest. It's a bummer, but this book can't do that. But it *can* lead you to the One who can pull off such an operation.

Lion-hearts are rare these days. Men and women with wild and holy abandon are so few nowadays as to be confused with being non-existent. But there is a reason that you, my friend, are holding this book in your hand and why you are hearing this message. Could it be that you are the stuff of legends and God is saying to you right now, "It's time, My son, My daughter. Rise up and live this life like you really mean it!"

⁂

I know a young man named Chad who is in desperate need of tagging along with you and listening in on our conversation. But it seems Chad is still not yet ready for what's in this book.

Chad is searching for something—a sense of meaning, a conquest, a cause. Ironically, he's searching for what is inside this book and simply doesn't realize it yet.

Chad is 26 years old, single, and completely self-absorbed. He spent the entirety of this past weekend in San Diego at a Star Wars convention. But there is something stirring within Chad that all of us can relate to. We want to be a part of something bigger than us. We want to feel strong, powerful, effective, and honorable.

But for lack of a better outlet for this deep longing within Chad, he has turned to a stormtrooper costume and a world of imaginary play-acting. And when he dons his Imperial armor, he feels, even if it is just momentarily, that he is a player in a vast and significant drama—he feels a sense of power, a sense of purpose, and a sense of importance.

Monica, a 24-year-old fantasy-gamer, is good friends with Chad. The two share a common angst for the boredom of life and a common love for the imaginary realm. Listening to the two of them talk would be absolutely hilarious if the evident emptiness of their lives wasn't so palpable. Monica thinks Chad's love for dressing up like a stormtrooper is ridiculous. "Goofy idiocy" are, I believe, her actual words. But, here's the irony. While Monica chides her buddy Chad for the whole stormtrooper gig, she thinks spending nearly 18 hours of every given day playing *Everquest* online and living out the heroics of a digital warrior is a completely valid way to spend her existence.

My heart aches for Chad and Monica, and I desperately long for them to enter into this discussion. Because Chad and Monica, if they only knew, could become players in a vast and significant drama that is actually *real*.

The first thing I want you to know before you arrive here at Loodles is that this book is not metaphor, hyperbole, or tantalizing fiction. This book is about real life—a version of real life that most of us long ago gave up believing really existed. This isn't about play-acting knights, samurais, or Jedis. This is about being made mighty, courageous, important, and noble *in actuality*.

The second thing I want you to understand is that it will take guts to read this book and follow its prescription. And I'm not talking the kind of guts that leads a person to parachute out of an airplane, bungee-dive off a cliff, or ride a mechanical bull. This is the kind of guts that goes beyond the human macho variety. This book will stare you in the face and say, "If you want this, which I know you do, you are going to have to relinquish life as you now know it…and choose to never return."

To enter this conversation, I want you to first grab ahold of your God and plead for heavenly guts—a strength that is not your own, a muscle that comes from a different realm, a steel of soul that the everyday version of humanity around you simply doesn't possess. *Because you will need it.*

If you want what is packaged inside this book, then you can't coddle self anymore. You can't get weepy with self-pity and mushyhearted with self-defensiveness. When truth speaks you are going to need to let it speak and let it change and alter you into something new and different. Great men and women are not made great by chiding truth and attempting to reconstruct it so that it is more appealing to their selfish sensibilities. Rather, they are made great by bowing down before the God of the universe and yielding to His commands and His methods for changing this world.

Now, there is one more thing I feel is imperative to communicate before you arrive and settle in for our conversation. I guess you could call this my battle speech. It might not move you quite like William Wallace shouting, "All men die, but few men ever live!" but I hope it strikes that one nerve in your soul that is desperately longing to be plucked. I want to let you in, from the beginning, on my vision for this generation of mousy men and women.

Nearly 6000 years have passed since Adam was first fashioned in Eden's garden. If a generation is defined as 40 years, that would mean *many* generations have come and gone since the genesis of creation.

Every age of history has boasted heroes—great and mighty men and women. Every generation is measured by the quality, the durability, the strength, and the character of these heroes. As the heroes and the mighty in a generation go, so goes the generation.

There have been some extraordinary generations of heroes. In fact, the list of these generations would make up a who's-who in mighty humanity throughout history. And the men and women in these hallowed generations were real, and the battles they fought were real. They didn't need to imagine the conflict stirring about them. They didn't need to shimmy into a stormtrooper costume, or pick up a battery-powered lightsaber to feel alive. All they had to do was open their eyes and breathe in the real world about them to feel the electricity of being an honest-to-goodness hero with a real-life cause.

If all the generations since creation were congregated together before the bar of heaven and before its divine scribes, there would be little debate over which of the generations would rank as chief and captain over the rest. There have been seasons of history when mighty heroes arose, devastated the powers of hell, and flexed the muscles of the mighty King of heaven. However, even the most illustrious of generations must hush and bow in humble veneration when the two mightiest of the mighty generations stand up and take their places in their seats of antiquated honor.

For there are two generations that stand regally apart from the entire host of generations whenever the topic of the *most mighty* enters the conversation. There are two generations that boast the strongest of the strong, the mightiest of the mighty, the bravest of the brave.

I must admit—as a man, I am transfixed with admiration when I behold these two generations, and you will soon discover that this book will, consequently, spend its vocal chords in singing the praises of these two glorious ages of mighties. For these two generations hold the architectural blueprint for what is known in history as the Holy Gibborim, or the Company of Heroes. These two generations boast the sacred pattern for the construct of *Wrestling Prayer*.

What's amazing is these two generations are mirrors of each other even though they are separated by over 1000 years. And as a result of their uncanny similarities to one another, I refer to them by the same name, and I am moved to speak of both with hushed tones and reverential deference. To me, they are simply called the Times of the Mighties, for they represent the greatest seasons in history when the most mighty heroes of history roamed the Earth and performed the most amazing and inexplicable exploits. These were the seasons of greatest valor, greatest honor, and greatest glory. These were the centuries when the kingdom of God was established and the Earth shook with wonder and awe at the devotion of the few who performed supernatural feats and literally accomplished the impossible before the onlooking world.

As a man I long to participate in the Times of the Mighties. I yearn to be transported back in time and have the Almighty integrate me into the rich, death-defying, world-altering drama of history.

But here's the war cry of this book:

Leslie and I yearn to see *our* generation become a mirror of these two most heroic ages. We want today's generation to gain a name amongst these two most mighty generations of heroes. I wish for the bar of heaven and the divine scribes to hold this current unfolding generation in the highest esteem and declare, "It truly became one of the most mighty!"

And yet here is the grave dilemma. Too many of the men today are mice, not men. Too many of the women of our age are vain, not valiant. We are paranoid of battle, not productive in it. We are soft where we should be solid, and hard where we should be soft.

Every voice within us may declare that such a generation of men and women cannot emerge out of this current congregation of lambs. Every indicator in this natural realm may mock the ambition of this book, but Leslie and I have fire in our souls; we have an unquenchable longing to see the fame of our Jesus restored and the power of His gospel reinvigorated in His limp-wristed people.

God desires to call forth out of this generation a mighty battalion of ready and eager soldiers. We beg you, as you prepare to sit down and enter this discussion, to ask yourself this question: "Am I willing to be counted among the mighties?"

Up to this point, our generation has offered very little substance with which the Great Cloud of Witnesses can stand and cheer. Where are the men? Where are the women? Where are the heroes? Where are the blood covenanters? What happened to the Company of the Mighty? Please, someone tell us that the Holy Gibborim will rise again out of the polluted ashes of this current generation.

Are we to be termed the Generation of Mice, or is it possible that we might rise to such a title as the Generation of Legendary Heroes? If it is even a remote possibility, then we need a greater cause, a greater purpose, a greater drama with which to fill our lives.

Yes, we realize that our passion may sound a bit overdramatic for such a pathetically boring age as ours. But our energies to write this book are not stimulated by culture, but by Christ. We are transfixed upon the glory and the majesty of our King Jesus, and we fully expect to spend our bodies and blood in seeing the rightful King of Earth be honored as such. And until His sacred beautiful feet touch down on Mount Olivet and the mountain splits in half—until every knee bows and every tongue confesses that Jesus is Lord, until He takes His seat upon the throne in the New Jerusalem here on Earth, His heavenly robe fills the temple, and the River of Life gushes forth from beneath His Kingly seat—until that day, our swords will not rest, our prayers will not cease, our passion cannot and will not dim.

You may not feel very mighty right at this moment, but we pray that our conversation will prove to be a genesis of newfound strength and purpose within your soul. For the very essence of wrestling prayer is a mighty disposition.

Please feel free to take a sip from your frothy concoction, for once we start talking you may forget that you are in a coffee shop with a mocha in hand. It is our prayer that you will feel transported into a different age, a grittier time, and that you will feel the ancient winds of Judea rush through your hair, the dust of Bethlehem between your toes, and the scent of a fire from heaven in your nostrils.

For Leslie and me, the content of this book is a living coal from the altar. It has dramatically altered our lives and has ushered forth a new power, energy, and confidence to our daily walk with our Lord. It's more than a book about *how* to pray; it's a book about how to live the Christ-infused existence and how that causes one to become a spiritual wrestler. It's not a how-to book about prayer, per se, but more one to mightily move you to pray.

You may wish to buckle your seat belt, because it's quite possible that what you are about to read may shake you to the bedrock of your existence.

As I said in the beginning, a conversation at Loodles is not what you'd expect. It's serious business. For we are headed to the rolling pasturelands of Judea, where amongst the sheep, the boasting giants, and the hurling rocks we are going to learn wrestling prayer from the very best to ever walk this earth.

Leslie and I wish you Godspeed.

# *a moment for prayer*
## BEGINNINGS

≈§ LESLIE §≈

As I mentioned in the introduction, at the end of each chapter we are going to take a brief interlude from all the exciting manly stuff that Eric's been dishing out and get practical with all these grand thoughts. After all, what good is truth if it isn't liveable? If you can't put epic ideas into practice in normal everyday life, then it really doesn't matter how nice they sound—they aren't very useful.

Eric and I are committed to ideas that actually work in this real world. We are after a Christianity that isn't just triumphant in word, but in action. And that is what this book is really all about. It's about being triumphant in action.

God has commissioned us to fight for the truth of the gospel, the pattern of the kingdom, and the glory of the King—but most of us stare blankly back at God and shrug our shoulders, saying, "But I don't know how to fight!"

Soldiers fight with bullets and bombs, boxers fight with punches, talk show hosts fight with words, and politicians fight with power and social leverage. But we are supposed to be of a different manner than this world—our fight is a different one and our method of fighting is very unique: it's prayer. And that is why we must know how to wield this nuclear weapon. For when prayer is used properly and in accordance with the heavenly pattern, then storms are calmed at our command, mighty empires fall to the ground in a heap of rubble,

27

powerful giants thud to the Earth, lame men rise up and walk, fire thunders down out of heaven to consume the altar, water turns to concrete beneath our feet, food is multiplied, and the heavenly chariots of fire become visible to the naked human eye.

In these first few chapters you may wonder to yourself, *Isn't this supposed to be a book about prayer?* But soon you will see that to know how to fight, we must first know what it is we are fighting.

We'll start to get more practical at the end of the next chapter. But I do have one practical piece of advice at this point in the journey: pray. Take a few moments and dedicate this experience to God. Ask Him to speak to you through the pages of this book, to awaken you to truths from His Word, and to infuse you with the supernatural ability to become a mighty warrior for His kingdom. And if you pray that prayer in sincerity, watch out! You are in for one amazing adventure.

So let the battle begin…

# THE PLAGUE OF THE GIANTS
*begging the faith of a five-year-old*

⇥ ERIC ⇤

I believe the Bible to be true—the entire thing, from cover to cover. Now I mention this belief due to the fact that there is a vast crowd of modern Christians who simply don't buy the biblical account. It's not that they don't think it is fascinating, inspiring, morally motivating, or ethically grand—it's just that they say it's not very believable. As my friend, a self-acknowledged Christian philosopher named Brian says, "I read parts of the Bible and I'm like, 'Yeah, right!'"

Let's look at the short list of "yeah, rights" that a supremely intellectual man like Brian can compile from the first few pages of Genesis:

- A woman made out of a rib. Uh-huh.
- A snake who talks. Okay.
- A man who lives 969 years. Really?
- A guy spending 100 years building a boat the size of a football stadium. Hmmm.

If you are one who is prone to fantasy adventure, this is good stuff. However, if you are one of those stiff intellectual types, like Brian, who prefers your worldview to fit within the bounds of natural reason, then the beginnings of Genesis can prove an awfully big stumbling block to the old faith-o-meter.

I happen to be a guy who loves logic and rationale, I have a fetish for things making sense, but I also, without the slightest hint of contradiction in my soul, wholeheartedly believe the biblical account to be true. Call me crazy, but to me the whole thing makes total sense. Unlike Brian, I have absolutely no problem with the fact that it says Eve was fashioned out of Adam's rib. Why should I? To me the Bible isn't a collection of exaggerated tales and fantastical adventures. It's raw truth, it's unvarnished history, and it's a stunning picture that there is a God that rules in the affairs of men. To me, the Bible lives and breathes. It's a book with a personality, a voice, and a power to invade the human soul and move it to action.

The Bible proves that God doesn't just acquiesce to bend this natural physical realm to bring about His purposes, but that He actually delights to do it, and fully intends to do it. And it shows that there is nothing sweeter to the heart of God than to have the people of this Earth submit to Him and trust that He is a performer of all that He promises. He says in no uncertain terms throughout the Bible, "If I say Eve was fashioned out of the rib of Adam—just believe Me when I say it! I was there—*you weren't!*"

My friend Brian looked at me with compassion in his gaze the other day and said, "Ludy, I'll give you the fact that you are sincere—but you are sincerely foolish."

You might agree with Brian that I am intellectually inferior due to the fact that I take the Bible at face value and simply believe it, but what you may not understand is that my simple trust in this sacred book is one of my secret sources of strength. For this ancient book is mighty, and when you approach this mighty book with the simple confidences of a little child, the might stored within its ancient pages somehow transfers itself into the human soul and invigorates it for heroic living.

So, if you are an intellectual who thinks himself smarter than the Word of God, I hope my unwavering confidence in the Bible doesn't prove a stumbling block but rather an inspiration as you keep reading. For what we are about to enter into is sacred territory that can be apprehended only through the wide, believing eyes of a little child.

This divine terrain holds untold blessings in its bosom; however, those blessings will be gleaned only by those who rise up and claim them with the unabashed faith of a five-year-old.

This is a book about the mightiest men who ever walked this Earth, but this might cannot and will not be had by those who put their confidence in their own strength, their own ability, their own intellect, and their own pedigree. This is a might of divine origin, of heavenly impartation, and it is obtained only after first becoming weak.

It's sad, but my friend Brian flat-out refuses to read this book. He decries it as "fables and mythologies." And as a result, Brian will not possess the grandeur contained herein. However, if you are willing to enter into this near-unbelievable story of the divine empire of God with a childlike frame of mind, I can promise you, your intellect will never be sharper and your consciousness of the grand adventure all around you will become clear and steadfast for the immense battle of souls waging about us.

Many historians have chosen to act as if the Jewish Holocaust never happened. And yet, it did. Whether we acknowledge the great and near-unbelievable stories of history past as real doesn't change the fact that they were.

I'm hoping you took me seriously back in chapter 1 and buckled your seat belt, for we are about to cross the threshold into the Times of the Mighties. These are two generations full of the most inconceivable stories history has ever known—two generations of men who lived and breathed the impossible, the power of Jehovah God and, as it says in the Sacred Book, "did mighty exploits." These were human beings like you and like me—normal everyday men. But they were men who spent their lives for history's most important cause, and as a result they were imbued with something *super-normal* and they lived lives that were wholly inconceivable—lives that many throughout history have chosen to dismiss as exaggerated and overly fantastical.

The stories this book declares are stories I believe with all my heart and mind to be true. So I appeal to the five-year-old within you to rise up, grab five smooth stones, and head out, right alongside me, into the Valley of Elah—for it's time to pick a fight.

✥

Genesis 6:4 is a classic stumbling verse for intellectuals like Brian. It starts by saying, "There were giants in the earth in those days."

"Giants?" Brian huffs incredulously. "Are you saying, Ludy, that you actually believe this stuff to be literal?"

But it is the second half of Genesis 6:4 that really gets gooey and uncomfortable for the naturalist: "And also after that, when the sons of God came in unto the daughters of men [in other words, had sexual relations with them], and they bare children to them, the same became mighty men which were of old, men of renown."

Yes, yes, Brian, I realize that this sounds rather fantastical—angels of God having sex with earthly women and producing the mighty men of ancient times. This is certainly "Yeah, right!" material.

I have no desire to try and explain this bizarre historical account here (as if I had the slightest clue) any more than I wish to attempt to explain how physiologically a man's rib can be fashioned into a woman. There are some things I just don't understand and don't need to understand. But that doesn't stop me from believing them.

Now the reason I bring up this obscure Scripture reference to start out this book is because there is something very important found in it that affects the rest of our journey together.

God has a dynamic and extraordinary intent for His creation, His people, His bride (the church), but throughout this ancient drama Satan is hell-bent on disturbing God's plans and thwarting this sacred intent. Satan is interested in polluting the race of men, of distorting their true intent, and weakening them into mere slaves of his depraved regime.

I must admit, he hasn't done a shabby job.

God created human life and called it good, and Satan's goal is to warp that human life so that it no longer can be deemed as such by the Almighty. He wants to turn its loyalties away from God and to himself.

From the time Adam and Eve were deceived in the Garden of Eden, Satan has proven himself to be quite the military tactician. He knows his opponent well and he wields a myriad of the most cunning stratagems, which are all aimed to undermine and weaken the strength of his nemeses. And what this odd passage of the biblical text in Genesis 6:4 unveils is that Satan, in the first centuries of Earth's history, was able to build an army of dark heroes, a race of giant men to propagate his evil agenda upon this Earth.

Those of us raised in Sunday school know that Satan has been in the business of twisting and warping humanity since the Garden of Eden. And as Jesus says in the New Testament, Satan sits in the seat as "the prince of this world" (John 14:30). Somehow this evil character holds sway over the masses in Genesis 6:4, and he sends his emissaries out to the "daughters of men" seeking to actually impregnate them with the seed of his diabolic agenda. And it's not just those strange historic giant men who were born as a result of this tactic, but this satanic warping of the human race has found its way into our modern DNA as well. For, at a certain level, we are all born of this "prince" with an instinctive loyalty toward his kingdom agenda, toward sin.

And as it says in Genesis 6:5 (which by the way, is immediately following this emergence of these bizarre giant men), "God saw that the wickedness of man was great in the earth, and that every imagination of the thoughts of his heart was only evil continually."

Satan had successfully baited men away from their true Prince in heaven and now men everywhere, all throughout the Earth, were casting their crowns at the enemy's detestable feet and essentially declaring to him, "You, O Lucifer, are my rightful prince."

And not only this, but those who were still loyal to the crown of the Creator were now the hunted and the despised amongst the Earth, for Satan had masterminded this race of giant men to carry out his bidding and to destroy the remaining loyal children of the Creator.

This is the pattern repeated over and over again throughout history.

Satan raises up his giant men, and the Earth quakes beneath the weight of Satan's boastings and sway. The world grows dark with wickedness, and it would seem evil itself has become incarnate in and through the hearts of men on planet Earth. But such are the times of the greatest men and women. For this is when the most mighty are called upon to perform their exploits, to remove the stain from the renown of God, and to fight to see the evil prince dethroned and the true Prince take His seat in holy Jerusalem.

And so it was in the Genesis drama, for it says, "The Lord said, I will destroy man whom I have created from the face of the earth...for it repenteth me [it stirs in me great sorrow] that I have made them."

And then listen to this great and telling line in Genesis 6:8:

> But Noah found grace in the eyes of the Lord.

Every time the darkness has grown so thick and the giant men of Lucifer have formed a seeming impenetrable barrier to the establishment of the Creator's kingdom, God has found His champions, such as Noah, who were willing to risk it all for the sake of the Almighty's glory.

The word in the ancient Hebrew for these giant men was *Gibborim*. It simply meant "the mighty men." However, these Gibborim are *not* to be mixed up with the Holy Gibborim mentioned in chapter 1. These mighty men of Lucifer were half-breeds, half-angelic, half-earthly savages. They were huge, stalwart, brilliant, courageous, and demonically inspired soldiers. And their task was simple—*destroy the people of God.*

And there is a sense in which these giant men of Lucifer still march this Earth today. Oh, they don't come clothed with armor and spear and stand a towering nine feet tall. Satan isn't stupid. Whereas in the past he bluffed and boasted with the size of a human footprint and the sheer strength of a human muscle, he now bluffs and boasts with the subtlety of a new and modern race of mighties. And whereas they might look different than the ancient race, their task is precisely the same: absolute annihilation of any and all loyalists to Christ's crown.

Now before you gulp and give sway to fear, let it be known that God's people have never been destroyed and they have never, for one instance, needed to back down to this physical display of power. In the darkest and most desperate of times of Earth's history, God has raised up His very own band of mighties to take on the legions of savages. In Noah's time He raised up only one. But Noah, God's Holy Gibborim, stood undaunted in the face of the host of Lucifer's finest, and defeated them all by simply obeying his rightful Lord and entering into an ark made of shittim wood.

This book is about prayer, yes, but it's about the prayer, the fight, and the growl of God's Holy Gibborim—men who are real-life men, yet men who are more than just men as we know men to be. They are holy hybrids—in whose skin, God, the Most Mighty One, lives and moves and has His being, performing His brave and noble exploits in and through the yielded obedience of sacred living.

The order of the Holy Gibborim is as ancient as Earth itself, and its pattern for wrestling heroes hasn't altered or changed in even the slightest degree from the beginning. It's the pattern of the Most Mighty Himself, who, as the very Creator Jehovah God, donned the garment of human skin and strode onto the stage of time to show forth His Almighty power and remove the head of hell's greatest champion, the one known as Lucifer. With the dauntless swagger of heaven, the Most Mighty hung as a naked bloody pulp of seemingly defeated human flesh before a legion of Lucifer's bloodthirsty giant men, and under the guise of apparent weakness, He reached out His hand and stripped the evil army of savages of their source of strength and left them eternally impotent.

The Holy Gibborim are heroes constructed by God, built by God for the glory of God. It's a version of human living that breathes love, justice, and sacred passion with every breath. It's a grandeur of soul that demonstrates the handiwork of the mighty carpenter from Galilee.

Do you long for such a sacred society to call you kith and kin? If you are feeling the tug upon your soul, and something inside of you is longing to know more, this book will aim to set before you the sacred blueprint of this rarified order of heroes.

I am about to lay out before you in this book the secrets of the Holy Gibborim. But, please beware: If you approach these secrets as a stiff intellectual, you may miss them altogether. However, if you approach them as a five-year-old, the vestibule of heaven awaits.

# *a moment for prayer*
## FAITH

~3 LESLIE 3~

M y mom bakes great homemade bread. Each loaf has that lus-
cious, bulbous, golden-brown sort of look, and they each smell
of heaven, glistening with buttery scrumptiousness. But no matter how
hard I try to imitate my mother in this culinary arena, my version of
her hand-me-down recipe never seems to turn out as good as hers.

Let's see. There's flour. Check. Water. Check. Yeast. Check. Baking
soda. Check. Salt. Check. Dough conditioner. Check. I whip the
whole collection of ingredients together, kneed it in my Bosch, let it
rise, stick it in the bread pan, bake it at 325 degrees for 40 minutes,
and what do I get? Holes in my bread. Aargh!

A lot of us feel this way in our spiritual life. Commitment. Check.
Ten minutes of uninterrupted time. Check. Hands folded. Check.
Sweet angelic prayer voice. Check. Desire to see prayers answered.
Check. "Amen" placed at conclusion of long list of smart-sounding
requests. Check.

We jam all these ingredients together a couple times a week, mutter
our long list of smart-sounding requests for ten minutes, stare up at
the ceiling in hopes of seeing manna fall from the crawl space, and
what do we get? Holes shot in our expectations. Aargh!

So many of us are defeated in our prayer life before we ever even
get started.

"I tried praying like that," people say, "but it just didn't work for me."

"Prayer is a bit overrated," others mutter. "God knows how much I love Him—I don't think He needs me to tell Him a whole bunch of things He already knows."

So many of us have tried whipping up a quick batch of bread somewhere along the line in our Christian life, and it didn't turn out very well. Our souls said, "Aargh!" and the pain of the disappointment still lingers inside us. And as a result, we've thrown the whole concept out so that we don't end up with unmet expectations or our hopes once again dashed against the rocks of disappointment.

But for many of us, we need to start again. And this time, with a different recipe—one that was handcrafted by God Himself.

Many of us have had spiritual leaders who have given us faulty recipes for prayer—recipes that lead to precisely this sense of defeat and discouragement that so many of us feel.

We need to throw out the tepid and tame renditions of praying and inject the fight, the fervor, back into the whole operation.

When I bake bread and forget the salt, it doesn't mean that what I remove from the oven is not bread. It *is* bread. But it is bread that doesn't taste quite right.

In many ways that is precisely what has happened to the majority of our modern-day recipes for prayer. They are missing some key ingredients and they have had counterfeit filler materials thrown in to compensate for those ingredients.

## A Recipe for Wrestling Prayer

Let me give you a quick peek at the recipe for prayer that Eric and I will introduce you to throughout this book. I think you will find that it only vaguely resembles much of what many of us have been surrounded by throughout our lives.

The recipe for true wrestling prayer mixes an ample supply of faith with absolute abandon to the Spirit. It combines a healthy dose of spiritual swagger with a truckload of tenacity. Then it blends together several generous servings of focus, holy aggression, and heavenly audacity.

That's one confusing list for those of us who grew up in the domesticated and unenthusiastic modern church. In some ways, it's like exchanging out the water and the salt in the recipe for bread for Tabasco sauce and horseradish. It's adding some serious heat to the experience.

These are the ingredients that, when combined rightly by the blazing Spirit of God, changes the world and alters history.

Most of the items on the list above are somewhat foreign to many of us. But the lead ingredient sounds a bit familiar: *faith*.

In the last chapter, Eric said, "What we are about to enter into is sacred territory that can be apprehended only through the wide, believing eyes of a little child. This divine terrain holds untold blessings in its bosom; however, those blessings will be gleaned only by those who rise up and claim them with the unabashed faith of a five-year-old."

Faith is confidence, assurance, all-out trust that someone who said he would do something will in fact do it.

My little boy, Hudson, doesn't squirm with doubt when his Daddy promises him that we will go to the zoo when he awakens in the morning. He trusts Daddy's promise, without question, without hesitation, and lays his head on the pillow with delight and unmitigated enthusiasm squealing within his heart.

Scripture says that those who want to engage God and truly live as He has called them to live must *first* believe He is a rewarder of those who diligently seek Him. This is where it starts. We must *first believe*, and then everything else begins to come into alignment.

But therein lies our modern dilemma. We don't actually believe what the Bible says. Oh, we believe bits and pieces of it, but we don't actually believe that the living substance of the life of Jesus, let alone of Job, Moses, Joshua, Samuel, David, Daniel, Elijah, Elisha, Peter, James, John, and Paul, is intended to be planted squarely in the midst of our bodies and animate us to live lives likened unto theirs. We just don't buy it. We wriggle beneath a hovering doubt when notions of being victorious over our addictions, being freed from our lusts, or conquering our fears comes up in conversation. And we have no grid whatsoever for notions of walking on water, calming storms, giving sight to the blind, or seeing the dead raised back to life.

Why is it we can believe the Bible and believe God can do anything He wants, but we for some reason become sheepish and hesitant whenever the idea of God doing something huge is applied to our personal situations or circumstances?

What we call "faith" these days is, in fact, what Jesus referred to as *oligopistos*, or "little faith." It's not that we don't have confidence in our God to save us from hell; we just don't have confidence in Him to do everything else that He promised to do while we are still on Earth.

But this is where the mighty prayer life begins. The recipe calls for faith. And this is the real sort of faith—not the doubting, never-sure rendition that is served up with a chorus and an offering basket these days at your local church, but the kind that moves mountains and changes the direction and flow of history.

You may find that when you open the pantry of your soul to see if there is any faith there that you can stir into this grand recipe for prayer, that you are running seriously low.

But don't panic. Because if you panic here, it will only get worse when we start going down the rest of the recipe list. These are ingredients that are necessary for the prayer life that God has called us to enjoy, but we need to deal with first things first. We need to acknowledge that our pantry is, for the most part, barren.

Before we can start wrestling in prayer, we need to seek the elements that will help us wrestle in prayer.

So here are some practical things that you can do right now, today, this week, to begin to change the condition of your pantry.

## Faith-Building Exercises for Wrestling Prayer

> My life is one long daily, hourly record of answered prayer.
> For physical health, for mental overstrain, for guidance given
> marvelously, for errors and dangers averted, for enmity to the
> Gospel subdued, for food provided at the exact hour needed,

for everything that goes to make up life and my poor service, I can testify with a full and often wonder-stricken awe that God answers prayer.[1]

—Mary Slessor, missionary in West Africa in 1876

### 1. Find Stories that Build Faith

One of the best ways to build faith in Jesus Christ is to surround yourself with believers who are strong in faith—Christians who believe that God is as big as He claims to be, and have personally seen His power and faithfulness demonstrated in mighty ways.

During my teen years, I was deeply impacted by Krissy, Eric's sister, when she was fresh off the mission field. Krissy was full of amazing stories about how God had miraculously provided for her, protected her, and supernaturally brought souls into His kingdom. Hearing her accounts of God's faithfulness exposed my own low expectations of God—and as a result, I began to pray bigger prayers and see more miraculous things happen in *my* everyday life.

In addition to Krissy's modern-day experiences, I was also incredibly inspired toward a life of faith by reading historical accounts of great Christians throughout the ages.

History is filled with stories of mighty men and women who overcame impossible obstacles through faith in the power of their God. The problem is, in our modern day and age, we don't hear many stories that build faith. Rather, we seem to hear the opposite. The most popular books in the Christian market are typically those in which the authors talk candidly about their disappointment with God, their difficulty finding a real experience with God, and their grappling with the reality that God just doesn't seem as big as Scripture makes Him out to be.

Our faith will not be built by messages like that. Our perspective on the magnitude of God's power will not be strengthened by singing lackluster worship songs that focus on us instead of Him. One megachurch in our area is fond of using the U2 hit "I Still Haven't

Found What I'm Looking For" in their Sunday services. How can such mediocre meditations possibly convince us that God is with us, ready and willing to perform mighty works in our midst?

Instead, if we want to strengthen our faith-building muscles, we must flood our hearts, minds, and souls with reminders of the faithfulness and power of our God, and disregard all messages that speak anything else.

In Ephesians 1:19, Paul wrote that he desired us to grasp "the exceeding greatness of his power toward us who believe, according to the working of his mighty power."

God has provided mighty power for His children; He has called us to perform valiant exploits for His kingdom and His glory. But this power can be accessed only by those who believe. If you find it difficult to grasp the exceeding greatness of His power toward you, begin listening to testimonies that glorify the faithfulness of God. If you have heroic Christians in your life who have personally witnessed the power of God, meet with them and ask to hear some of their stories. And even if you don't know any faith-filled Christians, there are plenty of inspiring books and biographies that can build your faith through the testimonies of mighty men and women of God who have gone before you. Some of our favorites are...

- Corrie ten Boom—*Tramp for the Lord*
- Sabina Wurmbrand—*The Pastor's Wife*
- Amy Carmichael—*Gold Cord*
- Arthur T. Pierson—*George Muller of Bristol*
- Norman Grubb—*Rees Howells: Intercessor*
- Jackie Pullinger—*Chasing the Dragon*
- Howard and Geraldine Taylor—*Hudson Taylor's Spiritual Secret*

### 2. Keep a Prayer Journal—and Get Specific

Just this week a young Christian friend of ours told Eric, "I never pray for anything specific. I've always been told that if you pray for something specific and God doesn't answer it, you'll get disillusioned with God."

This is a typical attitude among modern Christians. We are afraid to get too specific with our prayers, because we are worried God won't answer us. It's far easier to pray vague, general prayers so we don't get our hopes disappointed.

But here is a crucial truth: *Specific praying is the key to building faith.*

It's the way Christ asks us to pray. (See Matthew 18:19-20; 21:21; Mark 9:23; John 14:12-13. James speaks similarly in James 5:15-16.) It's the pattern of Scripture. And when we are willing to go out on a limb and make a specific request of God, our faith grows as we see Him come through for us. One of the best ways to build your faith is to keep a prayer journal and write down specific prayers you are bringing before God. Then wrestle in prayer for them on a daily basis until the breakthrough comes. Record every answer to prayer, small or large, in your journal. Then, a few months or years later, you'll be able to read back over your prayer journal and see the faithfulness of God. Whenever I've kept a prayer journal and revisited it later on, I'm always amazed at how God demonstrated His power in my life—and my faith is built mighty and strong.

Eric and I have found that we didn't really understand praying until we began to pray specifically. As Charles Spurgeon said:

> There is a general kind of praying which fails for lack of precision. It is as if a regiment of soldiers should all fire off their guns anywhere. Possibly somebody would be killed, but the majority of the enemy would be missed.[2]

Our prayer journals echo the testimony of Martin Luther, who attested:

> No one can believe how powerful prayer is and what it can effect, except those who have learned it by experience. Whenever I have prayed earnestly, I have been heard and have

obtained more than I prayed for. God sometimes delays, but
He always comes.

If you keep a prayer journal and are daring enough to bring your
specific requests continually before God, this will be your testimony
as well.

# THE CORRUPTED THRONE
*silencing the rebel voice within*

Saul the king—the self-preserving ruler

⇥ ERIC ⇤

I remember complaining about life when I was 11. The summer break
from school was waxing a little long and I had made the fatal error
of announcing to my mother that I was bored. She assigned me a
week's worth of chores to forever cure my boredom, and it was somewhere in the middle of those days of "slave labor" that I pronounced,
"My life stinks!"

My mom consequently went on to inform me that there were
people starving in Bangladesh and that my trivial challenges paled in
comparison. I think I replied something akin to, "Being without food
sounds easy next to slave labor!"

It's amazing how easily self-pity can creep into the human life. It
can make a perfectly wonderful existence feel like a torture chamber
simply due to the fact that the milk you purchased from the store last
Tuesday went sour three days earlier than marked.

My mom had a self-pity detector in her right cranial lobe. She could
detect the ugly scent of the disease from three rooms away, the lights
off, and the vacuum running. For all of you who didn't have a mother
with a nose to sniff this bad boy out and have therefore gone through
life totally ignorant of its presence, here's a helpful definition:

**Self-pity** [self-pit-ee]—the juicy and oddly satisfying feeling that you personally are the most unlucky, unfortunate, and uncared for human on planet Earth; the very clear sense that you personally are getting a raw deal in life and that the universe (or in my case, my mother) is out to do you in.

It's amazing how many people spend a good portion of their life wallowing in this thing known as self-pity. Yes, I too have spent my fair share of time during nearly 40 years entertaining this insipid notion that "life is unfair," but, somewhere during those years I stumbled across a little-known fact:

Self-pity has destroyed more men and women than maybe any other vice.

Self-pity appears smallish, weak, and almost cute. It appears to be some harmless luxury of the human soul in hard times—but for all its seeming neutrality, self-pity has proven the conqueror of kings, princes, prophets, and mighty men throughout the ages.

Self-pity is no small force. In fact, the Holy Gibborim have long chronicled the vice of self-pity as more dangerous than the powers of lust to allure and the powers of greed to pollute—for self-pity is the little varmint that prepares the way for the other chief rebels of the soul. Self-pity sounds so benign, and that is why the Holy Gibborim call it precisely what it is—self-worship and self-preoccupation. The mighty men of old understood that self-pity is the father of all the other self-sins (self-indulgence, self-concern, self-applause, self-seeking, self-aggrandizement, etc.)—in short, *selfishness*. It's the doorway into the dungeon of Lucifer—it's the undercover spy of the evil regime sent to turn the soul of man from God-worship to man-worship.

Self-pity is not a thing to trifle with. To be hospitable to its charms is like experimenting with poison drops in your tea.

For all my mom's superhuman abilities—she wasn't omniscient (aka, all-knowing). At times I thought she might be, but as I grew older I began to realize that there were dark secrets in my life that she didn't seem to realize existed. In the Ludy home growing up, the "self sins" just weren't tolerated. But, like a lot of devilish little children, I found ways to beat the system. For instance, I realized one day that I could hide a little self-pity over here under my pillow, a little self-indulgence over here in my bottom drawer underneath my soccer cleats, and a little self-aggrandizement over here in my locker at school—and, get this: My mother would never know. My mother had an uncanny sensory ability to track down and expose the evil varmint of selfishness in my life. But, come to find out, I also had an uncanny ability to find ways to hide it from her.

A few years ago, a good friend of mine, a pastor, was over at our house for dinner and conversation. The topic of my old football and baseball card collection came up. I bragged about the fact that I had a world-class collection and baited him just enough to get him to say, "I'd love to see it!" I hadn't looked at my card collection since my high-school days, so I was quite intrigued as well to reminisce. I whipped out my "best of" album and started paging through it, my pastor-friend looking with curiosity over my shoulder the whole while. Lo and behold, as I turned the page to showcase my favorite card (my John Elway rookie year), a picture (ahem) of a scantily dressed young woman fell to the floor. I'm sure you could imagine my embarrassment as my self-indulgence from over a decade earlier found the light of day—in front of a pastor, of all people.

Mighty heroes are not made overnight. They encroach upon the hallowed halls of spiritual greatness one inch at a time, one step of obedience at a time. But there is one piece of the mighty hero puzzle that *does* happen overnight. And it involves the centerpiece of man's soul—the prize of the eternal realm.

The inner throne of man is what both the kingdom of Christ and the kingdom of Lucifer are after. And when this throne is yielded to the Almighty God, a man enters upon the sacred path of greatness right then and there.

The eternal realms are all about a throne. The destiny of a human soul depends entirely on who sits upon the throne of that soul.

Well, I yielded this throne of inner control over to Jesus Christ when I was 19. But what I didn't realize at the time was that I was, in a sense, inviting over 10,000 Mom Ludys into my inner life to labor full-time investigating my heart and mind 24/7 for any presence of self-sin. Every pillowcase examined, every dresser drawer culled, every last inch of my locker scrutinized, and every football-card album paged through and purged of all distraction.

"Dear God!" I remember thinking when this examination of my soul first began. "I can't handle this! Please, let me be!" The whole process was exhausting to my soul. I didn't realize how many crevices in my life had become strategic hiding places for secret sin.

"You must learn, Eric," God seemed to say in response, "I give no quarter to the enemy! I can provide no hospitality to the flesh. Your body is *My* house now, and you must allow Me to make it a place fit for a King's presence."

The architectural design that God follows in building His Holy Gibborim is deemed rather harsh by those of a "softy" nature. Many men and women throughout the ages have been flabbergasted with how intolerant and prejudiced this sacred blueprint appears. But this heavenly blueprint isn't intolerant and prejudiced toward people— just toward sin, the flesh, and self-on-the-throne. If something stands against the formation of the kingdom of God in my life, then God is intolerant toward it. He doesn't mince words. He simply says, "It's gotta go, Eric!" If something in my life is blockading this world from seeing His glory, then if I don't shoo it away myself, He'll grab a whip and drive it out for me.

If this sounds cruel and heartless, I unfortunately am not at privilege to apologize, because I didn't invent this pattern—*God did*. He obviously knows that we can handle a lot more than we realize in this boot camp season of life. And, to be frank, the reality is that this pattern of God is, in fact, the epitome of love and grace—it demonstrates the depths of our heavenly Father's kindness toward us. God simply loves us too much to see us ravaged by sin.

If my son, Hudson, had a cancerous tumor on his lung, as a father

I would deem such a tumor a threat to his life and I would seek a way to radically purge such a plague from his little body. And it would be my love for my little boy that would motivate me.

God's love for us is like a heat-seeking missile. It is ferocious and persistent in its pursuit of the human soul—to not just claim it, but clean it, and crown it with life.

A couple Saturdays back I was having breakfast with a young man here in Windsor. Between bites he asked, "Eric, would you mentor me?"

Without a second's pause I answered, "Absolutely!" Then after a brief but ponderous moment I added, "But just know, Eric Ludy will not give quarter to the flesh in your life!"

I have a passion for men to be true men; women to be true women. And I must admit, this sacred blueprint has spoiled me from ever being one of those mushy-hearted leaders ever again. I used to want my followers to like me, and now I find myself far more concerned about them being completely unhindered in their relationship with Christ so that they can truly become *like* Him.

Please be forewarned: This book will offer you no quarter to the flesh; it will give no reprieve to the self-preserving part of your soul. Yes, it will likely prove uncomfortable as a result, but as you will see, when the flesh is removed from its position of power, the human soul is made ready to usher in the glory of its true and rightful King.

~❦~

If you are ready, let's fly back in history to the time in Earth's great drama when the stage was being set for the rise of the Holy Gibborim. You may already know the story, but you might not fully understand how this ancient story from the past affects your life as a believer in the here and now. Amazingly, the following story is an active reality, replaying its grand and desperate events in the center of your very soul, even as you live and breathe in the present reality of our modern times.

Note: A critical thing for each of us to know and understand is that the ancient tales of valor, sacrifice, redemption, and victory in the Old Testament that played out upon the physical Earth with physical wars and physical swords and shields now plays out upon the spiritual inner terrain of the human heart, with spiritual wars and spiritual swords and shields. In the Old Testament it was a physical kingdom, in the New Testament it is an invitation into an inner kingdom, a human temple.

Some 2750 years after Adam, a man named Saul strode onto the scene. It says of Saul in 1 Samuel that he stood head and shoulders above the entire nation of Israel.[1] Saul was the king that Israel dreamed of having—he was tall, strong, valiant, and would certainly cause the nations surrounding to tremble with fear.

I'm sad to say that whereas Saul proved to be one of the most important characters in the ancient tales of the Holy Gibborim, he himself was not counted among the sacred order of the Mighties. In fact, Saul stood *against* the company of God's great heroes and proved to be their greatest nemesis. His inclusion in this book is not flattering, but it's essential.

Saul represents something that each of us must face, and it isn't flattering to us either. There is one in the spiritual land of Israel today (our human souls) that stands against the rulership of our rightful King Jesus. This "something" sits upon the throne of our lives with pompous arrogance and refuses to yield the reins unto the anointed and rightful ruler of the Land of Promise.

So let's look at the story of Saul and hopefully unlock the very first secret to the League of the Mighty, and thus, the first secret to wrestling prayer. For just like in the first Time of the Mighties, there is a throne in our lives whose ownership must be once and for all decided. And the history of the spiritual nation of Israel hinges on this decision.

⁓⊰⊱⁓

So as the Bible account declares it, Saul was crowned the very first king of Israel. At the beginning of 1 Samuel 15, we read that the prophet Samuel came to King Saul with a command from God: "Go and destroy the Amalekites! Give no quarter to the enemy! Destroy them all—every man, woman, child, servant, oxen, and sheep!"

"Whoa!" we find ourselves instinctively saying. "Loosen up a bit, God! If these Amalekites did something wrong, why don't we send over a few Israeli ambassadors to try and smooth things out before we hack these poor people to pieces? I mean, after all, God, couldn't You allow Saul to make a few speeches about peace and love before You send him off to waylay the enemy?"

What we don't realize is how dastardly these Amalekites were *and still are*. These people are the descendants of Esau, and it seems that their entire objective in existing is to hinder the nation of Israel. They are a thorn in the side of God's people. Not only was Esau a bad fellow, but it seems his progeny is of equal spite. And, as a result, God has vowed to "have war with Amalek from generation to generation."[2]

Well, as the story goes, Saul does go and destroy the Amalekites. But, he doesn't do it the way God asked him to. Oh, he kills all the really bad parts, but he decides to keep the best of the oxen and the best of the sheep alive. After all, they just may prove useful. He also decides to keep the king of the Amalekites alive. Then, just in case some Amalekite guy happens to return from an out-of-country trip to see relatives, King Saul can hold a knife to his king's throat and say, "Uh-uh, don't even think about trying to get even—remember, I've got your king!"

Saul isn't a stupid man. What he did makes perfect sense—from a human perspective. All in one day he has both increased the financial surplus of his country (sheep and oxen are valuable commodities) as well as created the ultimate self-protective measure against future Amalekite hostilities. It makes perfect sense, that is, to all of us who have the propensity to do the very same thing. But God wasn't pleased with Saul's actions as commander-in-chief of the Israeli armed forces.

The next day God sends Samuel to pay a visit to King Saul.

"I thought," Samuel states with a furrowed brow, "that God made it clear that you were supposed to completely annihilate the Amalekites?"

"I did!" answers Saul.

I can just envision Samuel cupping his hand to his ear and saying this next line: "Isn't that the bleating of sheep that I hear?"

"Well," Saul blushes, "I kept the best of the sheep and the oxen alive so that I could *sacrifice* them unto God."

Okay, let's stop right here. You see, this story is about far more than Saul, Amalekites, Samuel, and bleating sheep. This story is about you, me, and everything inside of us that blockades the life of Jesus Christ from being made manifest.

You and I are given a kingdom to steward. But like Saul, we are really merely butler kings to the agenda of the True King of Israel, God Himself. And as was the case with Saul, we are asked to "destroy the Amalekites." For the Amalekites represent something: They are an amazing picture of what is known in the New Testament as "the flesh." And the flesh is that reprehensible preference for self that lurks within every one of our hearts. It is that base and selfish instinct to preserve our own interests at the expense of God's interests. It's that part of me that, when I was 16, clipped out a picture of a scantily dressed model and hid it in my football-card album (the place I knew my mother would never look). It's devious, it's deceitful, it's self-indulgent. It's interested only in selfish comfort and will happily crucify Christ afresh to secure it. God also has another name for it—*sin*.

God knows that as long as the Amalekites remain in the land of Israel, the kingdom of Israel will be weakened and ultimately crumble. Likewise, translating that into the Christian existence, as long as the flesh remains alive within our lives, the kingdom of Christ within us will be weakened and ultimately crumble. In other words, God wants these Amalekites and this flesh dealt with not because He's some heartless tyrant, but because He profoundly loves His children.

Let's get back to the story:

Saul's disobedience in this whole Amalekite affair doesn't appear that awful to us, but to God it was a huge problem. In fact, it was such a big no-no that Saul was rejected as king because of it. The message is loud and clear in the Old Testament: "Give no quarter to the Amalekites!"

It seems that modern Christians have become an awful lot like our good pal Saul. We might destroy the grosser elements of the Amalekites within the corridors of our souls (that is, we aren't molesting, raping, selling franchises to adult bookstores, or practicing serial murder). But we have allowed the flesh to remain alive in and amongst the congregation of believers. And just like Saul, we have allowed it to remain alive under the auspices of "doing sacrifice unto God"! Do we actually think God is pleased with our celebrityism and hero worship within the ranks of believers, our sensuous "Christian" music concerts, our addictions to pop culture, our inventive and culturally sensitized modes of bringing the gospel to this world?

Do we not realize that Saul was rejected as king because he didn't completely purge the Amalekite filth from Israel? Samuel said to Saul, "The Lord has stripped the kingdom from you and given it to someone *better than you.*"

God entrusted the kingdom of Israel to a man who shared his like venom toward the Amalekites. *His name was David.* And God called David a "man after [His] own heart" (Acts 13:22). David detested the Amalekites, and God esteemed his pure and godly passion and crowned him as commander of God's Holy Gibborim in the age of the Mighties. David desired a purified kingdom, a kingdom set apart, fully cleansed of all that was hostile to the loving rule of the True King of Israel, God Himself.

Each of us has this "Saul propensity" within us. In fact, many of us have become experts in setting aside the best of the sheep and the oxen on a daily basis. "God will be pleased that I've spared these choice lambs for Him!" we declare. When in actuality, God simply desires obedience. He commands, "Remove this flesh completely from the premises of my dwelling place."

A word of warning: God gives no quarter to this Saul propensity. It is hostile to His agenda in the human life and His purposes in the construction of His mighty men and women. And when the David propensity (which, by the way, is the stuff of the Holy Gibborim) begins to make its way into the willing soul, the Saul propensity will do whatever it can to hunt it down and destroy it. *The two are at enmity.* They are both seeking to rule the human life and claim the throne of the soul, but only one of them is sponsored by God. The Saul propensity is about preserving self on the throne, while the David propensity is all about establishing Christ's rulership and control over the individual human life.

Read your Bible and you will quickly discover that we don't want to have the Saul propensity rule the roost in our lives. We do not want to thrust spears at the incoming King of kings (Saul tried to kill David numerous times). We do not want to oppose the rightful ruler of Israel (Jesus Christ) in our lives, in our homes, and in our churches.

We must not give quarter to this Saul rebellion, this Saul self-preservation, and this Saul self-glory. This flesh must be quashed. It can't be pampered, hugged, kissed, and coddled. It must be dealt a hard blow to the head. As Paul the apostle said in Romans 8:13, "If ye live after the flesh, ye shall die: but if ye through the Spirit do mortify the deeds of the body, ye shall live."

Paul said for us to "mortify" the flesh. *Mortify* means "to embalm." It literally is a picture of giving something no breath, no voice, no life, *no quarter.*

After the incident involving the Amalekites, King Saul spent the rest of his days furiously attempting to preserve the throne of Israel for himself. He was paranoid about David. He was haunted by evil spirits, he was badgered with fear and anxiety, and he was absolutely miserable even though technically he still sat on the throne.

This can't be our end too. It *must* not be our end. We must yield our throne to the rightful King. We can't be paranoid about the one "better than us" (Jesus Christ) coming in and doing the job on the Amalekites that we couldn't pull off ourselves.

Saul wouldn't yield his throne, and in the end he died a miserable and tragically ironic death. In a battle against the Philistines, Saul killed himself by falling on his sword (1 Samuel 31:4-5). But nearby, watching the whole miserable fall from grace was none other than an Amalekite. And so as Saul breathed his last, a man from the very race he allowed to survive, was stealing the crown from off his doomed head.

By keeping ourselves on the throne of our lives and allowing the Amalekites quarter in the sacred territory of our souls, we are merely setting ourselves up for a death at their hands and a removal of our inheritance.

David will be crowned king no matter what. It *will* happen. But may it happen *now* in our lives, and not later at our memorial service.

The pattern by which the Holy Gibborim are built is radically opposed to the whole notion of selfishness. It's simply not allowed inside the terrain of the soul. The Company of Heroes is trained, like my mother, to detect the whiff of selfishness from a mile away. And it is trained to yank its sword from its sheath and mercilessly hunt down the furry demon of the flesh and put it to death without a moment's hesitation.

We, as modern-day believers, must realize that the ancient secret of David must become our secret too. For it's the secret of the vibrant Christian life, the secret of a truly efficacious prayer life.

We must give no quarter to the flesh and all his cunning cronies. We must draw our swords and silence in our lives this worm-tongued counselor. We must no longer lend our ears to its self-stroking advice. We must duct-tape its mouth and no longer listen to its doubting rants. And we must give it absolutely no quarter, no condolences, and no pity. It is a lying snake, hell-bent on keeping us on the throne of our lives, and thus itself in charge of our existence.

We read in 2 Samuel 1:1, "Now it came to pass after the death of Saul, when David was returned from the slaughter of the Amalekites..." What an amazingly vivid contrast is created here: While the corpse of Saul is being plundered by an Amalekite, David was out slaughtering them. I say let's be men after God's own heart, like David. Let's make sure we are the ones slaughtering the enemy rather than the ones being destroyed by it. (Please note: I am referring to slaughtering our *spiritual* enemies, not our physical ones.)

Let's not ever forget that Jesus picked up a whip, entered His Father's house, and did a little heavy-handed housecleaning. Jesus is very interested in the purity of His temple—and just to remind you, we are *that temple*! And Jesus declared that this temple was to be *a house of prayer* for all nations.[3]

⚜

Now as unpleasant as it might have been to start this book by discussing Lucifer's evil race of giant men or King Saul's fetish for keeping the throne of Israel, it was all very necessary. To become a mighty man or woman of prayer you first must realize that you are currently in hostile territory. There are enemies to your soul (Satan, sin, and the flesh) and these enemies are surrounding you, they are in your very ranks, and, in the case of sin and the flesh, are even inside you.

And to start out this great adventure into the hallowed archives of the Holy Gibborim, let's allow the prophet Samuel to come to us and say, "The Almighty requests that you destroy the Amalekites!"

Your life is all about a kingdom, and true prayer is all about a kingdom. And this kingdom is not your kingdom, but Christ's kingdom being established in your very body. And the secret of David must become your secret: Remove the enemies of Israel from your life, show them no pity, and destroy them and preserve your body for your rightful King.

And thus, you will become a house of prayer for all nations.

# *a moment for prayer*
## REMOVING THE ROADBLOCKS

### ◦❧ LESLIE ❧◦

So let's get down to the business of prayer.

The greatest threat to your prayer life isn't the devil. It's not some external force, some harassing demon from without. Surprisingly, the greatest threat to the powerful life of prayer is none other than *you*— it's self *within*.

Men and women left to their own desires, their own designs, always atrophy and fall into disrepair and ultimately self-destruction. It's been proven hundreds of millions of times throughout history. Einstein proposed it in the first law of thermodynamics, and all he was doing was reiterating what God made clear thousands of years prior in the Bible.

We, as humans, don't know how to better ourselves—we only know how to be selfish and, as a result, hurtful, harmful, and (for lack of a better word) *human*.

But there is one thing in the universe that can turn this whole human problem around. There is one thing that can reverse this trend and actually make humanity work as God intended—to grow, thrive, and become more and more perfect with the passage of time.

Let's just call it "the God factor."

Jesus came to this Earth with an expressed purpose, and that was to purchase Himself a people. To gain for Himself a bride, a body through which He could demonstrate His profound love, His astounding grace, and His triumphant power.

He came to make rebels into loyalists. To make self-centric criminals into Christ-centric wrestlers for His glory.

He came to make His church, those who would believe on His name, those transformed by His Person and His presence, and turn them into houses of prayer for all nations.

This is God's destiny for you. His will for your life isn't converts in the Congo or orphans in Liberia (though you may very well give yourself to these causes)—it's that you would be transformed into the image of God's Son, Jesus, and that, like Him, you would become a spiritual rescuer.

This is what prayer is all about. It's about doing the rescue work of Jesus here on Earth. Prayer, in a nutshell, is "kingdom business." God desires to build us into His workforce and then set us about the Father's business. And though the Father's business has many dimensions, the job of all jobs is to pray.

You see, in God's economy, things on this Earth don't change through wishing, through positive thinking, or through good karma. They change through faith expressing itself in loving fervent prayer.

God's people are commissioned to ask, to seek, to knock, and to plead that the realities of heaven be made reality down here on Earth.

So, to pray or not to pray. This is the question of life on planet Earth.

Prayer is the life function of those given to the kingdom of Christ. It's the job description not just of a few in the ranks of His heavenly order, but of every single man, woman, and child that call themselves by the mighty name of Jesus Christ.

But there is a rebel part of your being that detests prayer, that seeks to avoid it at all costs, that gets extremely tired at simply the notion of it. This is what the Bible refers to as the flesh. And this flesh is the greatest, most formidable enemy of prayer.

If the flesh is allowed to remain active within the believer's life, then the life of prayer will be snuffed out. Prayer is a God-activity; it functions off of God-fuel, and the flesh pokes holes in the tank of the Spirit-life so that the fuel drains dry and thus the engine of prayer can't turn over.

I want to warn you up front. Wrestling prayer is not easy work. In fact, it's work that goes against the grain of our natural bodies. It's taxing to our minds, hearts, and bodies, and therefore it needs supernatural impetus to come to life.

So, when you diminish the flesh and give your focus, your time, and your attentions to the life of God within you, then suddenly a wind begins to blow into the sails of prayer.

So let's get practical about diminishing the flesh.

## Yield to a Different Voice

First Peter 4:2 tells us that we should no longer live the rest of our time "in the flesh to the lusts of men, but to the will of God."

Romans 8:1 says, "There is therefore now no condemnation to them which are in Christ Jesus, who walk not after the flesh, but after the Spirit."

First Peter 2:11 exhorts, "Beloved, I beseech you as sojourners and pilgrims, abstain from fleshly lusts, which war against the soul" (NKJV).

All throughout Scripture, we are told to yield to the voice of God's Spirit rather than the voice of our flesh. To most of us, the term *flesh* is just an outdated, vague word that we don't really understand. But like Eric has said, *flesh* is just another word for *self*—our selfish, put-my-own-wants-first side. Many of us don't even realize we have a selfish, fleshly side. We make decisions based on our whims and desires. We do what makes us feel good. We follow our selfish wants. It's easy to live as a slave to our flesh without even realizing it, especially if we go to church and spend time doing spiritual things.

Our culture, even our Christian culture, has a tendency to encourage us to listen to our fleshly side. *Follow your heart! Pay attention to your emotional needs! Don't just meet everyone else's needs—take time for YOU! What do you want out of life? How can you fulfill your destiny? Live your best life now!* This kind of thinking gives a huge stage to the voice of the flesh in our life. Whenever your focus is on doing what *you* want and making *yourself* feel good, you can be confident that the Spirit of God is not the one leading the way.

The Bible makes it clear that if we yield to the flesh, we cannot yield to the Spirit of God. The flesh wars against all the things of God—and it must be silenced in order for us to deny self, take up our cross, and follow our King.

As Ian Thomas so eloquently said,

> The Christian life can be explained only in terms of Jesus Christ, and if your life as a Christian can still be explained in terms of you—your personality, your willpower, your gift, your talent, your money, your courage, your scholarship, your dedication, your sacrifice, or your anything—then although you may *have* the Christian life, you are not yet living it.[1]

Contrary to what our culture insists, this life is not about us. It's about Him. And only when we silence our selfish side can we truly excel at the art of wrestling prayer. So how do we learn to yield to the Spirit instead of fulfilling the lusts of the flesh? It starts with simple, everyday decisions.

For instance, your morning alarm clock. Do you yield to the beckoning whisper of Christ's Spirit, asking you to get up and spend time with Him, or listen to your selfish desire to stay in bed? Our entire day is filled with those kinds of decisions. We can either claim this life as our own, and do what our flesh desires, or we can deny self, take up our cross, and follow Him. The more we yield to His Spirit, the more we are able, by His supernatural grace, to live the pure, holy, set-apart life He has called us to live.

Daily life is filled with hundreds of choices to either give in to selfish whims or yield to Christ's Spirit. But most of us are so used to obeying the commands of our carnal desires that our ears are deaf to the Spirit of God. Silencing our selfish side takes a lot of focus and a heavy dose of supernatural enabling grace. But Christ is more than interested in equipping us to put to death the desires of our flesh.

When you woke up this morning, did you think of your day as belonging to you, or Him? Did you live as if your time and decisions were your own, or His? Did you allow the distractions and allurements of this world to turn your head, to occupy your thoughts, or to dictate your choices? Or was He your sole pursuit? How did you spend your free time? Doing what *you* felt like doing? Or pouring out your life for Him?

Every Christian struggles with selfish habits that need to be remade by the Spirit of God. Allow His Spirit to open your eyes to any part of your daily existence in which you typically yield to your selfish whims and desires. You may find it helpful to write down anything He brings to mind. Then, pray specifically for the grace to silence your selfish side in each of these areas, and begin putting it into practice in your everyday life. (For example, choosing to respond joyfully when your alarm clock goes off, instead of lazily pushing the snooze button or angrily hurling the clock across the room.)

It may take a few days, weeks, or months for those old habits to fully die. But if you allow Him to retrain your daily decisions and enable you to deny yourself, pick up your cross, and follow Him, you will soon understand from firsthand experience what Paul meant when he said, "It is no longer I who live, but Christ lives in me" (Galatians 2:20 NKJV).

## Ignore All Those Clever Excuses

Whenever we attempt to take a step forward in our spiritual life—especially when it comes to prayer—our flesh begins bellowing loudly. "Oh, come on," it argues, "it's so extreme and unnecessary to spend a lot of time praying. Just pray for a few minutes. God will still hear you. And then you can watch a movie or read a book. Doesn't that sound like a lot more fun?"

Our flesh can be a brilliant debater at times. I've heard so many young Christians offer excuses for why they are not able to give much time to prayer.

"I would love to pray as much as you and Eric do," one young woman told us, "but I have so much going on in my life. I have a job. My friends and family expect me to spend time with them. I have school. It's just not realistic."

"I don't set aside time in my day for prayer," another young man told us, "because I used to be legalistic in my Christianity. If I start getting a regular prayer time in my day, I'm afraid it will just become a legalistic thing I do, rather than something genuine. It's better if I just pray whenever I feel like it."

I am sure that to both of these individuals, their arguments sound logical and even wise. But these excuses are merely the voices of their flesh—cleverly disguised as "common sense" or "spiritual wisdom."

Here is an easy way to recognize the voice of the flesh in your life. Any voice that convinces you to take the easy way out (rather than denying selfish wants, taking up your cross, and following your King) is the voice of the flesh, no matter how wise or clever the argument sounds.

> *I'm too busy to pray right now—I've got urgent responsibilities that need my attention.*
>
> *I'm too tired to pray right now—doesn't God know how hard I've been working this week? I need a little downtime!*
>
> *I'm too distracted to pray right now—I've got this huge problem in my life, and I just need to get my mind off it for a while.*

Any of the above sound familiar? Yep—it's your flesh, screaming at full volume, doing whatever it can to prevent you from taking a step forward spiritually. These excuses may sound harmless. But Paul reminds us in Romans 6:16, "Do you not know that to whom you present yourselves slaves to obey, you are that one's slaves whom you obey, whether of sin leading to death, or of obedience leading to righteousness?" (NKJV). In other words, whatever voice we yield to is the voice we are enslaved to. Listening to the voice of our flesh may give us a false sense of freedom—the ability to do what *we* want to do. But in reality, when we yield to the flesh, we become slaves to our own selfish, sinful wants—and soon we are so enslaved to sin that we cannot live a life that honors our King.

To excel in wrestling prayer, we must become slaves to God's agenda, and *not* the flesh.

If you want to get serious about prayer, you have to make a conscious decision to ignore all of those brilliant-sounding excuses. You have to choose to make prayer the highest priority of your life—no matter how your flesh screams in protest. Corrie ten Boom said it well: "Don't pray when you feel like it. Have an appointment with the Lord and keep it."

At first, ignoring the voice of your flesh and yielding to the voice of His Spirit might seem difficult and tedious. It's crucial that you do not attempt to silence the flesh in your own strength or willpower. You must rely on the supernatural enabling grace of God—to do in His strength what you could never do on your own. Ask God to equip you, by His Spirit, to ignore your fleshly excuses and take strides forward in your prayer life. It's a prayer He loves to answer.

The more you put this principle into practice, the quieter and quieter the voice of your flesh will become, such that God's Spirit is directing your life rather than the voice of your own whims and desires. And once you experience a life led by His voice, you'll quickly realize there is no other way to live!

4

# THE RENEGADE ANOINTING
*the secret strength of a giant killer*

David the king—the better man

⊰ ERIC ⊱

G reat men and women are a rarity these days. Sure there are a host of spiritually *average* ones in this world—you know, the kind of people who have a strain of integrity, a basis of godly character, and a general desire to please God. But "average" humans aren't the sort ever to be inducted into the order of the Holy Gibborim. The Holy Gibborim would never diminish the grandeur of their honor roll and stoop to the mediocrity and blandness that marks the lives of many Christians today.

Even the "great spiritual heroes" of our age, those wholeheartedly devoted to the cause of Christ, dedicating their entire lives to the purpose of furthering the message of Christ, are not always the stuff of the Mighty. I have spent the past 15 years of my life amongst these types of men and women. The spiritual "point men" of today (myself included) seem to be many degrees removed from the stuff of the Mighty Ones of history past.

In our Western world we are demonstrating a pathetic show of what God intended Christianity to actually become. Oh, our "Christian" version of righteousness these days has elements of might, degrees of honor, and pockets of grandeur in its form, but it's merely a kindergartner's scribble of the Christ-life and certainly not the trained spiritual artist's depiction.

But this book isn't about defeat. This book isn't about what we don't yet possess. It's about what we might possess if we were to abandon ourselves unto the Most Mighty Himself, and allow Him to overtake our lives, possess us with His very life and control, and demonstrate to this world precisely what a believer is supposed to look like according to heaven's definition. Many Christians today argue that even the greatest spiritual heroes of the Bible struggled with sin, continually wallowing between spiritual victory and spiritual defeat. "Just look at how David sinned with Bathsheba!" they say. Or, "What about the apostle Paul calling himself 'the chief of sinners'?" they wonder. "Who are we to expect a life of triumph when even those great men didn't have one?"

When Paul makes statements in Romans 7:24 like, "O wretched man that I am! Who will deliver me from this body of death?" (NKJV) it's easy to assume that Paul, like the majority of modern Christians, was weighed down by sin and unable to live triumphantly—at least not on a consistent basis.

But we must not fail to put Romans 7 in the context of Romans 6 and Romans 8, which clearly proclaim Paul's own victory and freedom from the control of sin's power that Christ purchased for us on the cross. Paul may have been the "chief of sinners" before he was redeemed by the blood of Jesus and transformed by the Spirit of God. But once the power of God overtook his existence, he was able to live a holy, upright, victorious, triumphant life after the Spirit, and not after the flesh—charging us to follow the same example. (See Romans 6:1-7,12-14; 8:2-3,9-13.)

The Bible says King David "did what was right in the eyes of the LORD, and had not turned aside from anything that He commanded him all the days of his life, except in the matter of Uriah the Hittite" (1 Kings 15:5). For all the emphasis that we modern Christians like to place upon David's sin of adultery and murder, sin certainly did not control his life or define his existence. In reality, the instance of David and Bathsheba was *one* stumbling amidst a life of shining, supernatural victory and uprightness.

Neither Paul nor David offer an excuse for us to say, "Well, they were defeated by sin, so I should expect to be too." In fact, the opposite is true. Both of these men offer an amazing picture of God's stunning, redemptive power—how He can take a weak, sinful, defeated life and make it into a shining testimony of His glory and holiness.

This book is a call unto your soul, begging you to reconsider your entire vision for why you are here on Earth, and asking you to recalibrate your version of Christianity to the Almighty's standard.

No, I'm not saying that it's impossible for a Mighty to stumble or fail. I'm not talking about a life of sinless perfection. But I *am* talking about a life marked by the full purchase of the cross—power over sin, triumph in our souls, purity in our innermost parts, victory over the enemy and the flesh, and heavenly valor in our daily existences. Everything in our natural mind might declare that such a life is impossible. But Christ said that "all things are possible" to them that believe (see Mark 9:23).

At the time of this writing, I am a man of 38 years. I esteem with every fiber of my being the model of living showcased inside the pages of this book; however, I have not yet graduated into the rarified class of God's Gibborim. I have not yet attained unto the sacred roll of the Company of Heroes. But, I will tell you with all sincerity that it is my greatest longing to one day be listed amongst these Mighty Ones.

I don't know where you are in your spiritual growth process. You might be a beginner in this whole journey; you might be a seasoned veteran with many years already under your belt. Ironically, this message might be more difficult for the seasoned veterans than for the newbies simply because the beginners are usually hungry for more, while the seasoned ones have often long ago decided that they reached the pinnacle of God's intent for their lives.

None of us are yet to approach the finish line in this great race. The pinnacle is Christ Jesus, and none of us have yet attained to that perfect standard. The vision for God-constructed living is so vast, so endless, and so far beyond the limited picture we have accepted in our modern Christian world these days.

So, what does a mighty man or woman of prayer really look like?

Let's begin to explore this concept. Let's get introduced to the Holy Gibborim themselves and, in the process, ask God to train our souls in a like direction.

⁘

I first learned about the biblical character David when I was five years old. You know, the sheepherding kid who slew the mighty Goliath. I loved that story and used to act it out in my backyard. But all growing up, that great and entertaining story was never anything more than just a fictitious story made up of cloth figures playing out their fantasy drama on the stage of a really tacky-colored green board of flannel.

I don't wish to diminish the use of the flannel board or cartoon as a means of teaching young children. I can only assume that the flannel board and cartoons are probably a wonderful way to impart the knowledge of the history of Israel to little minds. But for some reason, when something is brought to the mind of a child in cloth and flannel or with cartoonish exaggeration, it has a way of emptying those ancient God-moments of their sense of authenticity and realism. Kids might learn facts through a flannel board or a cartoon, but I'm not so sure they are being brought into a sense of awe, wonder, and belief.

For those of you who still picture David as being a little five-inch-tall cloth cutout or a little vegetable named "Dave the pea," I wish to reintroduce you to this extraordinary real-life figure of history past. In the past ten years of my life, God has been re-introducing me to the historical—and very real—person of David. And what I've realized is that when you learn the life of David, it prepares you to understand the might and power of another King, an even greater King, known as Jesus.

David and Jesus—two kings, two captains, two deliverers, two men who inspired in their generation an army of warriors, a company of heroes, a legion of legendary lion-faced men.

As I said in the beginning of this book, there are two generations that stand apart from all the others throughout history. The generation of David and the generation of Jesus—these are the two extraordinary generations that make up what I am terming in this book the Times of the Mighties. These two generations were not hallmarked with the presence of merely one, two, or three striking heroes of Jehovah, but an entire army. And you must catch this point: David and Jesus were the kings who inspired this radical amassing of mighty warriors. It was David and Jesus who ushered forth this heroism out of the souls of what otherwise would have been ordinary men and women.

May it be so today in our souls. May we rouse ourselves as mighty men and women to rise up and abandon ourselves to the cause of our rightful King.

I deeply desire our generation to rise to such a sacred standard. May there not be just one, two, or three in our current generation that risk it all to scale this most holy mountain, but untold thousands. And, I'll make no bones about it: I want you to be one of them.

Some 2700 years after Adam's first breath in the Garden of Eden, God rejected Saul as king and God found Himself a different man for the throne of Israel—a *better* man. And this man was no ordinary man. He was "a man after [God's] own heart."

And when God commanded the prophet Samuel to find this man, He simply said, "He is of the house of Jesse in the town of Bethlehem" (see 1 Samuel 16:1).

*Bethlehem?* Does that sound familiar to you? Believe me, it is no accident that both of these great kings (David and Jesus) were born in the little town of Bethlehem. And you will soon find that that is not the only similarity this little shepherd boy had with our King Jesus, the Great Shepherd.

Samuel asked Jesse to bring his sons before him, for God had appointed one of Jesse's sons to be the next king of Israel.

Now Jesse had eight sons, but for some reason, he brought only seven of them to stand before the mighty prophet of the Lord.

David was the eighth son. The eighth! He was not only a lowly sheepherder but he was the eighth son. And his father, Jesse, didn't even think it necessary to bring him to meet the prophet. After all, there was no possible way that his littlest boy named David was to be the next king of Israel.

May this be an encouragement to your soul: Often, God's chosen ones aren't the ones packed with muscle and brawn, and the ones, like Saul, who stand head and shoulders above all of Israel. Our God does not build His mightiest warriors out of the stuff of flesh, but out of the stuff of willingness and desire. God esteems the inner yieldedness of a man and not the physical strength of a male or his ability to grow a thick beard.

God chooses Davids—the overlooked, the ones of lowly birth, the young men and women of a single-heart for God. The apostle Paul, for instance, wasn't a striking figure physically—in fact, many historical accounts describe him as a shorter diminutive man. But though he may have been shorter in physical stature, he was lionlike—full of power, full of courage, and full of passion for his King. He stood taller spiritually than any man in his day.

Samuel looked over Jesse's seven eldest sons and said, "Nope! God's chosen isn't here. Don't you have any more boys in this family of yours?"

I can just see Jesse squirm. I can see the seven eldest brothers grow cold with jealousy. And in one voice I can hear them inwardly groan, "No way! Not that little brat David!"

"Well," says Jesse, "there is one more, but he is out with the sheep."

"Bring him here!" booms the prophet.

David? Why David?

Elihu, Jesse's oldest son, was a grand physical specimen sure to woo the hearts of Israel to his cause. But God said, "No! He's not of the stuff of the Mighty!"

But come on...*David*?

He's just a young guy barely climbing out of his teen years—surely something is amiss here. Even Samuel is a bit confused over this turn of events.

*The eighth son?* Samuel must have thought. *God, are you sure You know what You are doing?*

And God says, "Man looks at the outside, but God measures the heart" (see 1 Samuel 16:7).

David had the right heart. It was the kind of heart that could be bent to God's agenda, that could learn to love as God loves, serve as God serves, feel compassion as God feels compassion, and feel hatred for the things God hates. David may not have been the strongest, the tallest, or the most esteemed of his brothers—but he was the one with the mightiest heart. David had the raw materials God looks for in His heroes—humility and childlike trust in God.

The next scene that unfolds is one of the most significant in the entire Bible. David arrives at the place of sacrifice where Samuel, his father, Jesse, and his seven brothers are waiting. He enters into the presence of the great prophet, and immediately Samuel knows that this eighth son of Jesse is to be the next king of Israel. And we read in 1 Samuel 16:13, "Samuel took the horn of oil, and anointed him in the midst of his brethren: and the Spirit of the LORD came upon David from that day forward."

This is what I term the "Renegade Anointing." This was not approved by the powers-that-be in Israel. Just a little reminder: Saul was still the king of Israel, and he wasn't very eager to give up his position. So I think it is safe to say that Saul wasn't backing this whole "let's pick a new king" thing unfolding in Bethlehem. In fact, when God told Samuel to go to Bethlehem and anoint the next king, Samuel responded, "How can I go? if Saul hear it, he will kill me" (1 Samuel 16:2).

This was a coup on the throne of Israel. The entire armed forces of Israel followed Saul's command, and here, right smack in the middle of Saul's jurisdictional authority, Samuel pronounces that Israel has a new king...and this renegade king is *a little boy* surrounded by jealous brothers and a father who didn't believe he was "king material."

Samuel says, in essence, "This little boy must defy Saul and his legions of loyalist soldiers. But this little boy is not without an advocate—God has given him His very Spirit to sustain him and strengthen him through the long battle, and to ultimately carry him to victory."

This is the pattern of the mighty: outmanned, outgunned, outlawed, with every conceivable obstacle standing in the way—and yet, nothing can stop God's Gibborim from achieving the destiny the Spirit of God has birthed within their boyish believing souls.

Do you still have your boyish (or girlish) believing soul? Or did you lose that treasure in this doubting, seriously faith-impaired world? Do you still possess that rare jewel of spirit that refuses to turn its back on hope and holds the cynical voice of man in derision, or are you swimming in the morass of unbelief? You may be the eighth son of Jesse the Bethlehemite, a boy of lowly birth. But do you believe that the God of the universe can usher you forth into His presence and call you to a high and holy destiny? Will you allow Him to pour out His oil upon your head and say, "You are My chosen one!"? Do you believe that the Almighty Ancient of Days can raise you up as a great and formidable believer, even though the odds seem to defy the very idea, and even though you currently are nothing more than an overlooked sheepherding kid?

If you have lost your boyish believing soul, it's not too late to get it back. It's not too late to say to God, "Make me little once again, dear Lord. Make me little in mind, soft in heart, trusting in soul. Please bring me back to that age of spiritual innocence when I simply believed that You are all-powerful and fully capable of doing precisely what You claim You can do."

This little shepherd boy named David believed. He simply believed that he was the king of Israel—he was anointed; it was done. His brothers, his father, and the rest of Israel may have sneered with disbelief, but this mighty-man-in-the-making knew it was true.

Was it yet true in the physical realm of nature? No, not yet. But in the heavenlies, it was accomplished; it was finished. And, henceforth from that day, David began to walk in the swagger of the freshly anointed.

There is nothing quite like the swagger of the freshly anointed. It's divine adrenaline pumping through the soul. It's pure and unwavering confidence that smirks at all opposition and whispers under the breath, "Nothing can intimidate me!" This swagger makes a man or woman unstoppable, unquenchable, and impervious to fear.

Very few believers in our generation have ever felt this sensation, this blazing reality of the Christian existence. But this swagger is ours for the taking. It's not pride, arrogance, or egotism—rather, it's feeling the courage of God fuse into your spine and the bravery of God flood your heart. It's a feeling of impenetrability, a sense of indestructibility, and a clear grasp on the reality that God holds you in the hollow of His almighty hand. It's as if your soul is captured in the solid resin of God's power and there is now a barrier of impervious grace encompassing your life. The enemy can pound upon this resin-enfolded life with a sledgehammer, yet the life inside remains untouched and unmoved.

It's a foretaste of immortality.

The God of the universe had declared David king of Israel. But he was, for all practical purposes, still just a shepherd boy. The multiple million Israelites who were his rightful subjects didn't even know yet that he existed, let alone that he was their king. And even David's family wasn't too sure about the authenticity of this whole "Samuel anointing" escapade. So, though David was the rightful king of Israel, his subjects were but a flock of sheep on the hillsides of Judea.

God's purposes for your life are grander than where you currently ply your hand. Your true trade is to rule and reign with Jesus your King. No matter how lowly or how highly you think about your current position in this life, you must recognize that you haven't even yet begun to come into your true career position. And you must, like David, apply the spiritual swagger to your life right now, where you live, where you breathe, where you labor.

David had a flock of sheep. And so David started being king of Israel right there with his little flock. He had to prove himself faithful with this little kingdom of responsibility in order that he would be prepared for the bigger kingdom of responsibility soon to come.

How did David steward this little kingdom of sheep? Well, as the story goes, a lion came and stole one of the sheep under his care. Whereas nearly every one of us as ministry leaders would have said, "Oh, it's terrible that I lost one of my precious sheep," this freshly anointed king of Israel, with spiritual swagger fully intact, ran after the lion, grabbed it by its hairy mane, broke its devilish jaws, and removed the helpless lamb from its teeth.

Who is this kid? He killed a lion, for Pete's sake…and with his bare hands! This is no mere shepherd boy. This is a king-in-the-making. This is a man who is jealous for those entrusted to his care. His sheep might not seem that important to all of us onlookers, but to him they were his most precious treasure.

If that wasn't enough, then came a bear who attempted to do exactly what the lion did and steal from David one of his precious flock. Did this bear not hear the story about the lion? Did he not realize this was no mere shepherd boy—this was the king of Israel?

"But he looks so small, so young," reasoned the bear. "Isn't this the eighth son of Jesse? Surely the rumor about the lion was a bit over-done."

But the bear soon learned that though this young boy was small, he was anointed with the Spirit of Almighty God and the mighty power of Jehovah coursed through his veins.

David ran after the bear, and with the same fierceness and unapologetic violence demonstrated on the lion, he broke the neck of the bear, cracked open his jaw, and took back what was rightfully his. And soon David was wearing a warm coat made of bearskin.

This is the swagger of the freshly anointed. Nothing intimidates this young boy—*nothing*! He is called to be king, so why should he fear a mere lion and a mere bear? He is called to be king, so if he behaves as the king he is certain God will preserve him as he performs his royal duties.

As I said earlier, this swagger is yours and mine for the taking. It's not something reserved merely for Old Testament shepherd boys—it's something that is efficacious for us modern-day Mighties-in-the-making as well. The same Spirit that caused David to break the jaws of a lion and a bear with his bare hands is the same Spirit offered to you and me through the purchase of Christ's cross. And the same Spirit that caused Jesus Christ to break the jaws of Lucifer's power and rip the keys of death from his beastly grip is the same Spirit that is prodding your soul right now and saying, "Let me have you, all of you, every inch of you!"

God's Gibborim are merely God's men and women who live with the spiritual swagger of their anointing. They are the ones who live in the reality of the power that they have been given. They are the ones who know what it is they have been called to and with fearless wonder they grab the manes of spiritual lions and break the necks of spiritual bears in proving that it is really true—they really are indestructible!

Yes, I will readily admit that this "sense of indestructibility" demands that you first possess the boyish (or girlish) believing soul. Without that innocent confidence in your heavenly King, you can be nothing more than a mere human, with mere human strength, fighting mere human battles, for mere human glory, and gaining mere earthly benefit.

But the God-empowered Gibborim are something altogether different than the paltry humanity of our age. They live supernatural lives, accomplish supernatural feats of strength and valor, and they stand fearless in the face of even the fiercest enemy obstacles.

David was a man constructed and empowered by God Himself. Just listen to the testimony of his own mouth regarding his extraordinary life and strength:

> For by thee I have run through a troop: by my God have I leaped over a wall...God is my strength and power: and he maketh my way perfect. He maketh my feet like hinds' feet: and setteth me upon my high places. He teacheth my hands to war; so that a bow of steel is broken by mine arms (2 Samuel 22:30,33-35).

These are not the confessions of a man who is merely a human-fueled warrior. Rather, these are the pronouncements of a God-constructed and God-empowered hero.

Now I started all of this by warning you that if you are "too grown-up" in your approach to the truths contained inside this book then you are certain to miss them altogether. This is a book for those who are young at heart, who have the spiritual eyes of a five-year-old and the simplistic faith of a little child. This stuff could easily sound like something out of a J.R.R. Tolkien epic.

The Holy Gibborim are not mere men; they are the King's men, equipped with a strength that is not of this world and a confidence that flows out of a holy oil-drenched interchange between them and the God of the universe on the hills of Bethlehem.

Don't be fooled into thinking that this swagger is too fantastical for our modern times. It's real. In fact, it's the essence of historic Christianity. This is the stuff of Jesus, the stuff of Paul, Peter, Andrew, John, James, Ignatius, Polycarp, and Justin Martyr. This is the stuff of Athanasius, Peter Waldo, Joshua Giavenello, Tyndale, and Wycliffe. This is the blazing inspiration behind Luther, Knox, Wesley, and Whitefield. The list of God's Gibborim throughout the last 2000 years boasts the greatest names and the greatest exploits. They were real men anointed by a real God.

This swagger carried men and women right into dens of demons, up onto bloody crosses, into arenas with hungry lions, to stand before kings and princes unabashed and unashamed, into concentration camps, to the gallows, and to the stakes to be burned alive. These mighty men didn't even flinch, and in the throes of death they grabbed the mane of the lion and the bear and broke their jaws. They were victorious even in their moment of seeming defeat, and they left the gawking masses wondering what it was that they possessed in their super-human souls—for it was not of this Earth.

Every last one of us is offered the anointing of David. We are all invited to that hill in Bethlehem where stands the mighty prophet of old. And if we prove a right heart ripened with boyish-believing confidence, the ancient prophet will dump that horn of oil out upon us and we too can partake of that heavenly swagger.

But it isn't just the same anointing that we are offered—it's the same training. We too are given the privilege of facing the lion and the bear. We are given the opportunity to prove the reality of our calling. Are we really sons of the Most High King, or is this just a fairy tale? We are given the chance to prove our swagger in this real world and see the reality of our indestructibility even while we are still sheepherders.

Like David, we may very well appear insignificant amongst the billions currently bustling about this Earth. No one really knows that we exist, let alone the fact that we are called to be amongst God's Gibborim in our generation. But even now, in our world of seeming insignificance, we have something to tend. God has entrusted us some sheep, and these sheep represent our training ground for greatness.

Ask God right now what your "sheep" are. Don't be surprised if He says, "Your soul, My son—start there! Guard your heart and your mind, My daughter—for this is My dwelling place!"

A swagger is a sacred, precious thing. If it is not applied then it disappears altogether. If it is never put to use on the lion or the bear then it disintegrates and empties of its power. A swagger unused is no swagger at all.

God says to all of us, "Put that swagger to use, My son. Test it. Prove it. Let Me build it, grow it, mature it into an all-out sprint!"

God gave David a season with his sheep in order that he would be prepared for his life as a mighty king. The lion and the bear were necessary proofs to his young soul that he indeed was an unstoppable, untouchable, unthwartable mighty man of Jehovah God. The company of heroes is shaped in private in order that they might prove the might of God on the open fields of glory.

The day came for David, just as it did for Jesus, when the great test arrived. This is a day that comes for each of God's great men and women. It's Omaha Beach, it's the Alamo, it's the cross. For David, it was the Valley of Elah.

David knew what it was to crush the jaws of a lion and a bear. So when the champion of Gath, the most dreaded warrior of Lucifer's evil band of giant men, stood in the Valley of Elah and blasphemed the armies of the living God, instead of trembling with fear, David rose up in indignation.

"Who is this uncircumcised Philistine, that he should defy the armies of the living God?" (1 Samuel 17:26).

David was incensed. He was still a boy not yet of fighting age, and yet that didn't stop him from thinking, *God anointed me king and this despicable giant is daring to mess with my flock!*

Every fighting man of Israel trembled at the sight of this warrior named Goliath, who boasted a height of over nine feet tall. But not David. He had already proven his swagger on the lion and bear. He knew he was untouchable and that anything he set his will to defeat would be utterly destroyed. He knew not only the power of his God, but the position his God had given him upon this physical Earth.

Do you yet know these things?

David arrived at the Valley of Elah that day to deliver food to his brothers, but that didn't stop him from announcing to the armies of Israel, "I'll fight the mongrel!"

When King Saul asked David where his confidence to defeat this evil warrior came from, David said,

> Thy servant kept his father's sheep, and there came a lion, and a bear, and took a lamb out of the flock...Thy servant slew both the lion and the bear: and this uncircumcised Philistine shall be as one of them, seeing he hath defied the armies of the living God. David said moreover, The LORD that delivered me out of the paw of the lion, and out of the paw of the bear, he will deliver me out of the hand of this Philistine (1 Samuel 17:34,36-37).

David was completely undisturbed by the imposing physical presence of this evil warrior. The very thing that caused every other warrior in Israel to grow weak in the knees caused David to rise up with outrage and holy hatred.

What do your knees do when Goliath starts barking and blaspheming?

We live amongst a generation of men and women kept in the dank prison chamber of Goliath. These men and women are his servants; he is their master. To some his name is lust and sexual bondage. To some his name is fear, anxiety, and timidity. Others know him as pride, selfishness, and control. He has many names, but to all those held hostage under the spell of his daunting physique he is soul darkness—he is despair.

And there are many of you reading this book who tremble beneath this giant's shadow of control. You have never felt that spiritual swagger that David demonstrated, but only the iron grip of lust, the shackles of fear, and the collar of pride. You know nothing of victory, only despair. And yet there is something in you longing to escape this giant's prison. You are longing to escape to Bethlehem, where that horn of anointing oil awaits, held in the ancient hand of the mighty prophet of old.

But who can defeat this champion of Gath? This evil warrior blasphemes the armies of the living God saying, "Ha! God's saints are impotent!"

This giant snarls and spits curses at the children of the Almighty, "You who claim the power of the cross are helpless to stop me! I can do with you whatever I like!"

Many of today's believers are despairing before the nine-foot-tall shadow of this menace. They have more confidence in the strength of Goliath than they do the strength of their deliverer known as Jesus Christ. But we mustn't listen to this mongrel's boastings. And we must, with boyish believing confidence, realize that there is a David in the camp of God who has said, "I will fight the mongrel!"

His name is Jesus! And this Jesus is not some five-inch-tall cloth cutout either. He is a real historical hero. He is a genuine man who lived and breathed upon the soil of this green Earth. And He is the conqueror of the Goliath of all Goliaths. For David was but a foretaste of the Most Mighty One who was to come. David defeated the physical Goliath, and Jesus conquered the spiritual one. And, blessed be His holy name, Jesus has broken the chains that have held us under this evil warrior's control and has called us all to join Him on the famous hillside of Bethlehem to be drenched in the very same anointing that He Himself had while walking this Earth. For He has filled the horn of Samuel afresh and is offering to pour it out upon us, that we too might swagger into that Valley of Elah and fearlessly conquer all who stand against His people.

He says, "Arise oh Mighties and conquer in the power of My name!"

There is absolutely no excuse to stay where you are at right now. If you are weak, He can make you strong. If you are timid, He can make you brave. If you are a pervert, He can make you pure. If you are selfish, He can make you selfless. If you are a shepherd, He can make you a king. If you are mediocre, He can make you a Mighty One of valor.

The Mighties down through the ages have been men and women who simply believed, with boyish believing confidence, that God defeated their slavemaster Goliath, and that He in so doing purchased that horn full of oil just for them. And with the wide-eyed enthusiasm of little children they, each one of them, journeyed to Bethlehem and found the mighty prophet of old waiting for them there. And when they saw Him they announced with childlike excitement, "Here I am, Lord!" And then they did precisely what their Jesus commanded them to do—they asked, they sought, they knocked. They each said, in their own unique way, "I need what's in that ram's horn—and I need every last drop of it!"

Do you have any inner demons? Does lust control you? Does it push you around and taunt you with its governance over your soul? Does pride have a hold on your mind? Are you under the foot of fear? The thumb of greed? The paralyzation of doubt?

There is no need to remain in these tiresome shackles.

Do you realize that these giants of darkness have been defeated? Let me repeat something supremely important: Do you understand that Jesus the Most Mighty defeated the Goliath of our souls?

It is finished!

The Most Mighty has set us free from these enemy soulcuffs, and

He is saying to each of us, "My son, My daughter, make haste to Bethlehem!"

All of God's Mighties are born in Bethlehem.

You say, "But I was born in Paducah, Kentucky! I haven't a chance!"

Do you realize that I am referring to a "new birth"? All of God's Mighties are men and women who are reborn. They once were ordinary, fleshly individuals—average people with average ambition accomplishing average things and enslaved like every other average Joe. But then they came to Bethlehem. And with that boyish (or girlish) faith bubbling up within their souls they sought out that horn of oil. And as that precious purchase of the cross, known as the Holy Spirit, came cascading forth out of that old ram's horn, a new vigor, a new mind, a new heart, and a new spirit awakened within these great ones. They were no longer ordinary, they were no longer average, and they were no longer powerless believers.

We are set free from Goliath's ancient and hideous power in order that we might stroll onto the open fields of glory and defeat the modern Goliaths in our generation. We are called as David was called. We are equipped as David was equipped. And we are preserved as David was preserved.

This is the essence of wrestling prayer.

We are to be the fearless ones, the courageous ones, the ones who stand when every other man sits, the ones who storm the gates when every other man turns and hightails, the ones who say, "I will fight 'em!" when every other man sinks in despair.

If you are game, I say, let us each journey to Bethlehem and be born into the bloodline of the ancient King of kings. The mighty prophet of old awaits with ram's horn in hand. Our King is asking for a few good men and women—men and women who are willing to spend body and blood for His glory.

I'm in! Are you?

There is a spiritual swagger for the taking. The question is: Who has the spiritual guts to claim it for themselves?

# a moment for prayer
## FORTIFIED FOR THE FIGHT

### ❧ LESLIE ❧

There is one line in the story of David and Goliath that jumps off the page at me. It says,

> It came to pass, when the Philistine arose, and came and drew nigh to meet David, that David hasted, and ran toward the army to meet the Philistine.[1]

I read this story quite a few times before this jumped out. And when you catch the picture of what is demonstrated in that one line, it unlocks the essence of wrestling prayer.

Notice it says, "When the Philistine arose." In other words, he was sitting. I picture Goliath in a lawn chair (an extra large one) being fanned by a host of Philistia's most lovely grape-feeding girls. Then it adds, "and came and drew nigh to meet David." When David saw that Goliath had arisen from his seat and was bringing the fight, he "hasted, and ran toward the army to meet the Philistine."

David hasted? So what does that mean? *Hasted* is certainly not an everyday word.

Well, "hasted" comes from the Hebrew word *mahar*, which means to move forth like liquid, to act with instant energy, to go swiftly like a charging lion.

When David saw the enemy making his move, he charged, and

before the lumbering giant knew what was happening he had a smooth stone planted deep within his forehead.

This is the sort of battle that God proposes. It's aggressive and heat-seeking. It doesn't just respond to fiery darts, it knocks those who are shooting the darts senseless. It moves forth like liquid, acts with instant energy, and charges with all the aggression and fervor of a lion.

This isn't how Eric and I have dealt with spiritual matters for most of our Christian lives. In fact, it's not even close. We've been busied in our ministry work, minding our own business, when meanwhile, the Philistine arises, comes, and draws near to us for battle. Then, while we are humming a sweet little tune of ignorance, a huge club clobbers us on the side of the head and we hear a roar of demonic jubilance in the distance. It's *then* that our prayer life begins. It's when we are attempting to pick ourselves up from the ground and dust off our Sunday best that we send forth our heartfelt prayers: "God, teach us to accept the things we cannot change."

I can't tell you how many times Eric and I have been waylaid by the enemy and our prayers were prayers of acceptance and fatalistic "Aw, shucks" while the enemy who hit us slithered off completely unmolested.

David "hasted." He charged into the battle. He was alert to Goliath's every movement and wasn't caught sleeping on the job. And though the enemy moved with hostile attempt to destroy him, he wasn't the one lying decapitated on the ground come the end of the fight.

Jesus also "hasted." He charged headlong into the fray. And when He cried out on the cross, "It is finished," it was. He had proven victorious in the most impossible battle, facing the most insurmountable odds.

You see, God doesn't lose battles. It's that simple. His men and women "hasten" into the battle, knowing full well that it may cost them their life, but also completely confident that they cannot lose.

We lose battles when we fight them in our own strength, in our own manner. But when we learn to fight (pray) as God does, there will never be a lost battle ever again. There will be times of seeming defeat, moments of great suffering, occasions of terrible loss, but there will never be defeat. Why? Because God doesn't lose battles. He always wins.

Why is it that David's confidence and his utter assurance in such a dark and forbidding situation feel so foreign to us modern-day believers? Because most of us have never felt that surge of supernatural confidence, that unwavering faith, in the face of our life's giants. We've never known David's anointing.

There is a reason that a lion doesn't cower before a rabbit. Because the lion knows its position, knows its strength, knows that a rabbit is not a valid threat. And there is a reason God doesn't cower before the powers of darkness. Because, like that lion staring at a little rabbit, God knows His position, His power, and His utter and complete sway over everything and anything.

But here's the problem: We feel more like the little rabbit staring back at the lion. We feel vulnerable, weak, and doomed. And in a sense, that's precisely what we are without God. We are helpless to stand against the enemy's attacks.

But the Bible says, "Greater is he that is in you, than he that is in the world" (1 John 4:4).

That's the equivalent of saying to a cute little furry rabbit, "Uh, you know, little rabbit, if that lion over there is bothering you, then put him in his place."

This is what David's anointing did. It took a mere rabbitlike shepherd boy and made him a lionlike giant slayer. It turned the tables on everything that was natural. And it caused a boy to "hasten" to the lion, grab him by the mane, and rip the prey from his teeth. Any normal boy would run from the lion, but this anointed one ran toward it.

That is wrestling prayer.

And this anointing is tantamount to making it happen. In fact, it's everything. Without it, we as believers are mousy, rabbitlike chitter-chatterers. But with it, we can turn this world completely upside down.

What David's anointing did for him in the natural realm, the infilling of God's Spirit will do for us in the spiritual realm. Lots of people say a "sinner's prayer" and assume they have the entire package of Christianity. But there is a big difference between a believer without Pentecost, and one who has been overtaken and filled with the mighty Spirit of God. Before the Holy Spirit came, Peter declared that he would die with Christ, but then the same night denied Him three times. Peter was willing, but his flesh was weak. He believed in Christ, but something was missing. No matter how passionate or zealous he was, he simply could not live the courageous, victorious, faithful-unto-death life God had called him to live. That is, not until Pentecost. But once the Spirit of God came like a mighty rushing wind and infused Peter with supernatural power, he was transformed from a fearful closet Christian into one who boldly proclaimed the gospel of Christ before the multitudes, at peril of his life, without even a moment's hesitation. He now had the anointing—the ability to live the life of triumph and superhuman strength showcased in God's pattern. Without God's Spirit, such things are impossible. But *with* God's Spirit—watch out, world!

*But I'm a believer,* you might be thinking. *Don't I already have God's Spirit? After all, I couldn't even acknowledge Jesus as my Lord and Savior without the Spirit, could I?* It's true that to even begin this transforming journey with God, we must have a measure of God's Spirit. But that's what we start with—a measure. Just like Peter, who obviously had a measure of the Spirit before Pentecost, there is still so much more God is waiting to impart to us. One of the most beautiful pictures of this in the Old Testament is the story of Ezekiel being led through the waters that flowed from the temple of God:

> When the man went out to the east with the line in his hand, he measured one thousand cubits, and he brought me through the waters; the water came up to my ankles. Again he measured one thousand and brought me through the waters; the water came up to my knees. Again he measured one thousand and brought me through; the water came up to my waist. Again he measured one thousand, and it was a river that I could not cross; for the water was too deep, water in

which one must swim, a river that could not be crossed (Ezekiel 47:3-5 NKJV).

In the beginning of the story, Ezekiel experiences the water only to a measure—it comes up to his ankles. But each time he is led through the waters, he experiences more and more of the river until he's actually swimming in it. If we've experienced a measure of God's Spirit in our life, we are to keep seeking more and more of Him until His life has literally overtaken us—where it's no longer we who live, but Christ who lives in us.

So how do you know if you are anointed? How do you know if the Spirit of God has overtaken your existence?

You know when wherever you walk, you leave the footprint of God behind you; whenever you talk, men are left trembling with the awe and conviction of a holy God heavy upon them; and whenever you "hasten" to the fight, giants fall senseless to the ground with an unearthly thud.

You know you are anointed when all those lions, bears, and giants that once struck fear within your soul now suddenly look a lot more like measly little rabbits.

Wrestling prayer demands that the one wrestling be anointed to wrestle. For as long as we remain rabbits, we will continue to be lunch for the lions. But when we are invaded and overtaken by the life of God and our hearts become His heart, our hands His hands, our minds His mind, and our vision His vision, we suddenly become effective. We, in truth, become as He was in this world.

Suddenly we are sharing in the confidence of God. Suddenly we are smirking at the enemy when he boasts his bogus strength and attempts to scare us with his seemingly magic tricks. Suddenly we are looking at life from God's vantage point, and, as it says in Psalm 2, "The kings of the earth take their stand...against the LORD and His Anointed...[but] He who sits in the heavens laughs" (verses 2,4 NASB). He scoffs at darkness. He holds lions, bears, and giants in derision. And so does the man or woman who has been anointed.

So how does this become practical? If the power of the Spirit is missing from your life, what should you do about it?

First, you have to believe it. And I know you may find yourself tripping over that point. But when you believe it, you will ask for it, you will seek it, you will plead with your God to meet you on the hills of Bethlehem with a ram's horn of oil in tow.

Pray and fast. Get serious in your pursuit of this. Close out everything else in life, if necessary, and make it the single aim of your existence. Because, truly, this is all that really matters. You need what only God has, and if He is giving it out, then you want to be first in line pestering Him, begging Him, grabbing ahold of Him and not letting go until you get it.

Jesus said, "Ask, and it shall be given you" (Matthew 7:7).

God needs men and women who can wrestle with the powers of darkness and not shy away. God is looking for soldiers who don't buy the enemy's bluff, bark, and show—but rather, are wholly convinced that the blood of the cross is able to defeat every foe.

So let's talk about what you can do right now, today.

**The Need to Remove Breaches**

The Bible describes the powerful account of Nehemiah, who set out to rebuild the wall around Jerusalem. The wall had been destroyed, leaving the children of Israel utterly defenseless against enemy attacks:

> The survivors who are left from the captivity in the province are there in great distress and reproach. The wall of Jerusalem is also broken down, and its gates are burned with fire (Nehemiah 1:3 NKJV).

What a perfect description of our spiritual lives! Most of us live in a state of distress, hounded on all sides by the enemy, and our defeated lives are a reproach to the name of Christ. There are no protective walls around us, and we are defenseless against Satan's attacks upon our lives. We go around nursing anger toward God for allowing bad things to happen to us, all the while forgetting that we have an enemy who is hell-bent on destroying us. And he will succeed as long as we leave our battle weapons untouched on the ground and the wall around our city in shambles.

But the good news is that God is ready and willing to help us build a wall of fortification around our lives and to give us every weapon needed to not just defend ourselves against Satan's schemes, but to storm the very gates of hell...and *win*. In Hebrews, we read about the heroism of God's faithful servants throughout the ages, and are told that "out of weakness [they] were made strong" (11:34).

They went from being weak and frail to being so strong in God's power that they could stop the mouths of lions and put armies to flight. It's that *very same strength* that God desires to work in each one of us. You may feel weak, frail, and vulnerable, but He is ready to make you stronger than you ever thought possible.

Nehemiah knew he would never succeed without the sovereign intervention and aid of the Most High God. It was an impossible task. And only God could accomplish it. The same is true of the fortification of our spiritual lives. Only with God's supernatural assistance can we successfully build a wall of defense against the enemy. But we cannot expect God to come to our aid if we have barriers of sin and rebellion standing in the way. The first thing Nehemiah did, even before attempting to lay the first brick in the wall, was to fast, pray, and repent of Israel's sins (see Nehemiah 1:6-9).

The reason the wall around Jerusalem was in such disrepair was because the children of Israel had turned from God. They had allowed their hearts to be wooed by other gods and they had forsaken their covenant with the King of all kings. And with every step of rebellion, the supernatural protection that fortified their city eroded, until their wall was in ruins and they were in captivity to their enemies.

If you are ready to become a fortified Christian, it is critical that you identify the breaches in your spiritual wall, and allow His Spirit to remove them. Corrie ten Boom explained it this way:

> If a Christian walks in the light then the blood of Jesus Christ
> cleanses him from all sin, making his life a closed circle and
> protecting him from all outside dark powers. But if there is
> unconfessed sin in that life, the circle has an opening in it—a
> gap—and allows dark powers to come back in.[2]

Prayerfully ask God to reveal any breaches in your wall—any sins you have allowed into your life, big or small. When we let sins remain in our life, such as lust, gossip, dishonesty, self-pity, or unforgiveness, we unwittingly allow the enemy access to hound and harass us.

Be willing to make drastic changes to your daily life in order to cut off enemy access points. For example, if you watch movies and TV shows that promote sensuality, you open the door for lust and sexual compromise to waltz right into your life. If you read magazines or surf Internet sites that feed the selfish cravings of your flesh, you open the door for materialism to take root within your soul. If you feed upon pop-culture messages, you open the door for selfishness and worldliness to gain a foothold over you.

God says we are to give no "opportunity" to the devil (Ephesians 4:27). Removing the breaches in our wall means removing all opportunity for Satan to access our hearts and minds. That is how we will be turned from fearful closet-Christians into mighty Davidlike warriors for Christ's kingdom.

Like Nehemiah, take time to repent of sin or wrong habits that God brings to your attention, and ask His Spirit to cleanse these sins from your life and close off all Enemy access points.

## The Results of Removed Breaches

As your breaches are identified and dealt with, you will find that your prayers are more effective, the Word of God is more alive, and your intimacy with Christ is more vibrant. Instead of constantly warding off enemy attacks, you will have two hands free to do battle for God's kingdom.

And remember, once you have brought a sin to Christ and asked

His forgiveness, He removes it from you *as far away as the east is from the west* (Psalm 103:12). If the enemy ever tries to hold it over your head again, stand firmly upon the reality of Christ's work on the cross. His blood has fully and completely covered it, and that sin is *no longer a part of your life.* When God looks at you, He does not see that sin. The enemy has no power or authority to torment you about a sin that is nailed to the cross. As the old hymn says,

> My sin, O, the bliss of this glorious thought
> My sin not in part but the whole,
> Is nailed to the cross and I bear it no more,
> Praise the Lord, praise the Lord, O my soul![3]

# THE SEASON OF CAVES
*joining up with the hunted and despised*

### ᲒᲔ ERIC ᲒᲔ

Never once does God go out of His way to describe any of His
Holy Gibborim as men of great stature and natural strength. In
fact, it seems that if anything, they were just your everyday normal
variety of men, made great not by the merit of their physical prowess,
but by God's presence in their lives.

Even such herculean men as Samson seem to have been but ordi-
nary-sized men imbued with superhuman strength.

I must admit, that I take great comfort in this fact.

You see, I'm not that impressive of a physical specimen. I'm just
over six feet tall, but I'm that classic "skinny" body type. If I eat a four-
course meal and layer on piles of clothing before I get on the scale I
might be able to crack 160 pounds. I'm not weak, but I also don't boast
the kind of strength that you might figure someone should have to be
writing a book like this one.

I've never been able to grow a beard due to the fact that there are
two spots on my boyish face that are just as smooth as a baby's bottom.
I have only one chest hair. Oh, and even though at the time I write
this I'm 38, I still get people thinking that I'm a teenager. I'll admit
it—when it comes to "mighty manhood," I just don't look the part.

This is why the story of David has become so important to me. In
my mind, I guess I sort of picture him built kind of like me. I always
envision him with a young boyish face and a single chest hair. He's

just kind of your average guy, with anything but an average heart. He's evidence of what God will do with a man fully given over to His heavenly agenda.

When coaches are building a basketball team, they look for tall men. When they are building an offensive line for the football team, they look for large men. When they are building the next aeronautical team for the upcoming space shuttle launch, they look for smart men. But God doesn't look at the same qualities that men do. He is interested in the willingness and softness of a man's inner life. *Is the man hospitable to the life of Christ?* It's that simple to God. He doesn't care if the man is tall, large, muscular, talented, smart, or wealthy— He only cares if the man is pliable to His holy agenda. God wants to know, "Is he available? Is he stretchable? Is he willing?"

God does not hesitate to take short, skinny, frail, uneducated, poor men and make them His point men (generals) in the battle of the ages. In fact, He prefers it, because when such men become mighty, the credit clearly goes straight to God Himself. There is no confusion over who built this man into such a picture of grandeur.

God's Gibborim do not typically look the part. Throughout history, there certainly have been large, strong, wealthy, and smart men on this sacred roll of honor—but these sort are far more the exception than the rule. God, for the most part, seems to prefer the obscure shepherd boy and unknown carpenter's son sort-of fellows over the blue-blood, muscle-bound, and supremely talented men of the age.

Okay, so it is clearly established that I don't look the part of a mighty man. And I have a hunch I'm not the only one that doesn't fit that "leading man" stereotype. So don't feel bad if you too might be struggling with envisioning yourself as having the makings of a bona fide hero in this generation. Let's admit it—it seems a bit arrogant on our part to assume upon ourselves such a destiny, doesn't it?

Why is that? Why is it that we shy away from the call of greatness, the extended hand of divine grace, the invitation into the hallowed halls of heavenly majesty?

I have been a frontline Christian leader for nearly 15 years now;

however, I have spent a good portion of those years shying away from lions and bears. I have seen more than my share of sheep consumed by the evil giant men of darkness—and I did nothing but whisper a mournful prayer, "Lord, help them." I didn't realize that God was looking for a man who would do something about it, who would dart after the spiritual miscreant, break his jaw, and snatch the prey from his teeth. I didn't know I could even be equipped to do something about lions and bears.

Now, I'm going to share something with you that many people would hesitate to share. I share it because you, as the reader, must realize that what we are talking about in this book is not theory, but actuality. And it has become actuality in my life.

I don't mean to say that it has become actual in my life, as of yet, to the degree it was for David. However, I am tasting the same "spiritual swagger" that he possessed. I have this "freshly anointed" reality coursing through my daily existence, and even if what I have today isn't the fullness of it, I have begun to realize it at a beginner's level. I have begun to embark upon the very first seasons of mighty-man construction.

About eight years ago I was beckoned from the sheep-fields to stand before the mighty prophet of old. And, it was then that I first experienced the oil cascade down over my being. The life and reality of the Most High God entered my being unlike I had ever known it before. And I've never been the same.

I have been a radical Christian for 19 years, but over the past 8 years it's as if my entire view of the world around me has altered. I know the power, the strength, the might, and the love of my God and I know that this power, strength, might, and love is mine to wield upon this Earth.

I guess you could call these past eight years, and especially the past two years, a "Bethlehem" season in my life. It's been a period of height-ened sensitivity to God's presence—a season of preparation. And I must admit, I've been experiencing the spiritual swagger of the freshly anointed. I have felt my hands upon the warm throats of lions and bears, and I'm finding out what it means to growl with the Spirit of Christ at work inside me. I'm finding that things that used to strike fear in my being have now become like insects beneath my spiritual shoe.

I've only just begun to understand this, but I can profess that once you have tasted the spiritual swagger it's impossible to give it up. When you can suddenly stare in the eyes of a hungry lion and know that he has nothing on you—it's exhilarating! When the bear community begins to distribute fliers warning one another to beware of you, there is a sense of indestructibility that awakens within the soul!

David stood against the greatest Philistine warrior and defeated him with one rock to the forehead. It says in the biblical text, "There was no sword in the hand of David" (1 Samuel 17:50). This kid took on a giant with the weaponry of a shepherd—a humble slingshot.

There is no doubt that David had something that I still am yet to attain. But boy do I want it!

David had a boyish certainty that as he stood up for God's purposes, God would stand up for him. And he proved this truth over and over again to the point where lions, bears, and giants became something to sneer at and laugh about.

After the giant fell to the Earth, we read,

> David ran, and stood upon the Philistine, and took his sword, and drew it out of the sheath thereof, and slew him, and cut off his head therewith. And when the Philistines saw their champion was dead, they fled (1 Samuel 17:51).

Many Christian men and women today are not of this order. We are told, "David ran, and stood upon the Philistine." This is wholly unfamiliar to our modern Christian sensibilities. You and I have grown up amidst a version of Christian living that cowers before giants. It attempts to explain why the giants of sin in our souls, the giants of powerlessness in the church, the giants of dysfunction in our families and marriages, and the giants of spiritual rebellion in our modern culture are still standing and why God *didn't actually intend* for us to contend with them and defeat them.

We have grown up around a rendition of Christianity absent of this Davidic swagger. *We aren't running to stand upon the neck of the defeated giants because these giants are still very much alive—and, to be honest, we greatly fear them.* The lions and the bears have stolen from the flock of God and yet many of the believers of our age have done nothing. David killed the lion and the bear, whereas too often Christians of our modern times run and hide from them. We have not been prepared for the Goliaths because we have failed the kindergarten of God's training (the lion and the bear).

The lion and the bear are elementary school training for the believer's soul. It's supposed to be the very first proving ground to prepare him for the nine-foot giants in the land. However, instead of following God's pattern of growing in ever-increasing confidence, it seems we are progressing in an ever-increasing cowardliness.

If you think it was impressive that David took on Goliath, just listen to how his confidence expanded throughout his career with the Most Mighty One:

> I will not be afraid of ten thousands of people, that have set themselves against me round about (Psalm 3:6).

He's not afraid even when ten thousand enemies surround him with venomous intent? That is the swagger I want! He knows his position in God. He fully comprehends the spiritual destiny marking his existence.

Just listen to David wax poetically formidable in Psalm 91:

> A thousand shall fall at thy side, and ten thousand at thy right hand; but it shall not come nigh thee (Psalm 91:7).

This guy understands the reality of his untouchability! He rests in the secret place of the Most High and therefore abides in the shadow of protection of his Almighty God. Whether it be a lion, a bear, a mighty giant, or ten thousand foes all at once—no evil can harm him and no evil can defend itself against his brawn.

Imagine such a reality! Imagine such a swagger being injected into your consciousness!

Again, listen to David boast of his position over the enemy:

> I have pursued mine enemies, and destroyed them; and turned not again until I had consumed them. And I have consumed them, and wounded them, that they could not arise: yea, they are fallen under my feet. For thou hast girded me with strength to battle: them that rose up against me hast thou subdued under me (2 Samuel 22:38-40).

Do you realize that this swagger is not creative metaphor? *This is real*—it's spiritual equipment not intended for use merely in heaven but upon this Earth as well, right now in our modern age. Through the conversion of covenants from Old to New, our modern battles are not primarily physical as were David's, they are first and foremost spiritual, but they are just as significant and death-defying. David had something grand and powerful—but what David had was actually dwarfed by what Jesus possessed and showcased while here on Earth.

David proved his swagger in the physical realm and proved God's power over the natural sphere. But Jesus went beyond even that. Jesus proved both His power over the natural and the supernatural realms. He had a swagger that strolled into a den of darkness far more formidable than the Valley of Elah—He ventured into hell itself and decapitated the power of sin and death.

David killed his tens of thousands, Jesus defeated His billions. David humbled and kept at bay the enemies of Israel; Jesus defeated every spiritual foe you and I will ever face before we ever even encounter them.

I would give anything to receive the same swagger that David possessed. But I am awed by the fact that Jesus has made not merely David's swagger available to me, but the very swagger of the King of all kings, the Master of worlds, the Ancient of Days.

Are you starting to catch the fact that we are a thousand miles removed from the reality of what we are supposed to possess as God's people? This swagger is the essence of Christ-constructed living—the impetus behind Christ-empowered praying. Without it, we are nothing more than limp-wristed poets who can pen sonnets of courage and victory but can't live out the first step of it in this real world.

Christ-constructed Christianity is the swagger of Jesus, the full-confidence of Jesus, and the victorious growl of Jesus planted into the bedrock of the soul.

I wish for you to feel the full gravity, the full weight, of your distance from this reality. Because only then will you be prepared to find it in actuality.

We've been sold a bill of goods that Christianity is nothing more than a man esteeming Christ to be King and believing in His atoning work upon the cross. But this is not all of Christianity! Christianity is a million miles beyond this! Christianity is passing from death to life; it's a new birth on the hillside of Bethlehem drenched in a heavenly oil. It's the reality of Christ's very existence, life, and power entering our souls like a rider on a white steed and claiming His throne for all eternity.

Jesus Christ—the rightful King of Israel, the rightful King of every human soul, and the rightful King of the entire universe, has received His anointing. It's accomplished. He *is* the King. But this anointing was a "renegade anointing." The horn of oil was poured upon His head in the heart of Lucifer's dominion—*Earth*. And Lucifer isn't giving up his position of control without a fight. The devil is powerless, yes. But he is powerless only to those who walk with the spiritual swagger of the King of kings. Lions, bears, and giants are nothing to those who recognize their power over them. But for the man unfamiliar with this swagger lions, bears, and giants will appear to be too powerful to overcome and he will cower before these defeated foes.

However, if a man or woman with unabashed boyish (or girlish) belief in the position and power of their King is willing to stand up against this Goliath and simply confess along with David that the battle is already decided—the proof will soon follow. Listen to David's heroic words of faith as he stood before the evil behemoth:

> This day will the LORD deliver thee into mine hand; and I
> will smite thee, and take thine head from thee; and I will give
> the carcasses of the host of the Philistines this day unto the
> fowls of the air, and to the wild beasts of the earth; that all
> the earth may know that there is a God in Israel. And all this
> assembly shall know that the LORD saveth not with sword
> and spear: for the battle is the LORD's, and he will give you
> into our hands (1 Samuel 17:46-47).

Look around you. Who is sitting on the throne in this earthly
natural system? It's easy for us to sing in our songs and claim in our
doctrines that "Jesus is on the throne!" And yes, this is true in the
heavenly reality. But just as David was anointed as king on the hills
of Bethlehem and it was settled in heaven, it wasn't yet realized on
this physical Earth (Saul was still on the throne that was rightfully
David's). There was a season of persecution that ensued until the realities of heaven became the realities of this Earth.

Here's the crux of this book; here's the crux of wrestling prayer.

The Mighties are for such a time as this. Our rightful King has not
yet taken His throne upon this physical Earth. Our rightful King, like
David, has not yet been recognized on this Earth as the rightful ruler
over all. Rather, His truth is in hiding, His people persecuted, and
there is a bounty upon all who would identify with Him. He is King,
yes, but His kingship is not yet recognized and His enemies have not
yet been made to bend their knees and confess His mastery.

Such is the time of the Mighties. And such is the time for wrestling prayer.

If there was ever a time to rise up and join our King, it's not when
He has entered into the fullness of His glory and all knees are bowed
unto His person. Rather, *it's now*, in the season of persecution. This
is when the true motives of the King's followers are proven. This is
the season of loyalty and love. *It's now*—in the hardest, most pressing time.

The Times of the Mighties are not times marked by earthly peace
and comfort, but great upheaval and great persecution. It was in such

seasons of persecution that both David's and Jesus's Mighty Men strode onto the scene of time.

David spent over ten years running and hiding from Saul. There were 21 biblically recorded assassination attempts upon his life during this time. He hid in caves; he was forced to receive food as a charity offering from those loyal to his ascension. He was hunted, and those who stood by him became the hunted right along with him.

To identify with David was to prove a traitor to the government of Israel. To stand with David was to stand against Saul. You could not stand with both simultaneously. To acknowledge David as king was to also die to life as one once knew it.

To identify with Jesus is to prove a traitor to the governments of this world system. To stand with Jesus is to stand against Lucifer, sin, and the flesh. You cannot stand with darkness and light simultaneously. To acknowledge Jesus as King is to accept death and to live as one of the hunted.

But here's the secret: When you stand with David, when you stand with Jesus, you are privileged to partake of their spiritual swagger. You are not left helpless against lion, bear, giant, and the forces of ten thousands—rather, you are equipped to become *more than* a conqueror. You are equipped to be a history maker, a world alterer, a giant slayer.

How?

*Through fighting, gritty, wrestling prayer.*

David started out a shepherd boy, the eighth son of Jesse, but he became a lion-killer. Then he became a bear-beater. Then he became a giant-slayer. Then he became the victor over tens of thousands. Then he became the deliverer of Israel. Then he became the spirit and soul of the mightiest men ever to walk the Earth (up to that point of history). Then he became the untouchable, unbeatable, indestructible, impervious, and swaggering warrior of God.

First Chronicles says,

> So David waxed greater and greater: for the LORD of hosts was with him. These also are the chief of the mighty men

whom David had, who strengthened themselves with him in
his kingdom, and with all Israel, to make him king, according to the word of the LORD concerning Israel (1 Chronicles
11:9-10).

It says of David's mighty host that they "strengthened themselves
with him in his kingdom." David was waxing "greater and greater"
and when these men left everything to join in the cause of David's
kingdom and his glory, they too waxed greater and greater into the
likeness, power, and indestructibility of their anointed leader.

Look at David's Company of Heroes and you will see David himself. They bore the emblem of his nature, the same passionate cause in
their lion-hearts, and the same spiritual power in their hands of war.

Among these Mighties were men who tore apart wild beasts with
their bare hands, destroyed hundreds single handedly, killed mighty
giants, and staved off the forces of thousands. They sound kind of
like David, don't they? These men were made like their commander.
They left everything for their rightful king, and their king imparted
to them his swagger, his might, and his heroism.

Likewise, look at Jesus' company of heroes, and you will see Jesus
Himself.

Jesus said to His most mighty before He left them, "Verily, verily,
I say unto you, he that believeth on me, the works that I do shall he
do also; and greater works than these shall he do; because I go unto
my Father" (John 14:12).

Jesus didn't just leave His troupe of Gibborim in the midst of hostile persecution without a hope or prayer. Jesus left His Company of
Heroes everything needed to wax greater and greater in the Spirit,
power, love, and grandeur of God. He left them His swagger. Jesus
lived the most mighty existence, the most perfect example of the
anointed man—and He said, "Follow Me!"

Paul the apostle, the chief and captain over Christ's New Testament Gibborim, said, "Follow me as I follow Christ."

This is the message to all of us mere humans in this mediocre modern
age. "Rise up! Follow your King! Partake of His swagger!"

Christ may not yet be revealed as King of kings to the cynical eyes of this rebellious world, but may He claim the throne of *our* souls and may we allow Him a beachhead of kingdom control starting with our very bodies, minds, and hearts.

He may not be evidenced as King on this Earth yet, but may He be evidenced as King of our lives. And may this Earth see the ruling power of our great Commander in and through our unabashed boyish (and girlish) belief.

And like the Mighties of old, may we usher forth the great ruling reality of God unto this Earth with the hallowed words, "Thy kingdom come, Thy will be done, *on earth* as it is in heaven!"

# *a moment for prayer*

## ASK

❧ LESLIE ☙

et's admit it. Life today doesn't feel very similar to life back in ancient Judea with all its criminal kings, nine-foot giants, and bloodied swords. And as a result, it's quite easy to feel a bit detached from all these biblical tales of valor. It's kind of like reading the Lord of the Rings trilogy and wondering what it might be like to be a hobbit with furry feet living in the side of a grassy knoll. Whether we like to acknowledge it or not, the biblical accounts feel a bit like fantasy.

This sense of nonreality that shrouds the biblical characters and their stories subconsciously has caused many of us to subtly (or sometimes, not so subtly) diminish their practical real-world value to us.

There is a reason the book of James goes out of its way to remind us that the prophet Elijah was a man just like us, of like passion, of like constitution, and a guy who lived and breathed on the very same Earth as all the rest of us (see James 5:17). For some reason, we need to be reminded of this fact.

Elijah called down fire from heaven; he prayed and it didn't rain in the land of Israel for three years; he outran a chariot in his old age; he was fed by ravens; and, if that wasn't enough, he was taken up to heaven (while still alive) in a chariot of fire.

That sounds more like a wizardy character in some J.R.R. Tolkien fantasy novel than it does a real-life flesh-and-blood human like you and me. But isn't that the point of this entire book? It's to wake us up from our suburban slumber and begin to realize that this pop-culture illusion that we all skip around in each and every day is not as real as what the Bible is saying.

It wasn't just Elijah, but also Abraham, Moses, Joshua, Samson, David, Daniel, Elisha, John the Baptist, Peter, James, John, and Paul that were built of the same stuff that we are. Each one of them lived and breathed in the very same reality that we share. They weren't fantasy characters in some theocentric novel, but were everyday people that God built into mighty heroes simply because they believed.

And here's their earthly report card:

> Who through faith subdued kingdoms, worked righteousness, obtained promises, stopped the mouths of lions, quenched the violence of fire, escaped the edge of the sword, out of weakness were made strong, became valiant in battle, turned to flight the armies of the aliens (Hebrews 11:33-34 NKJV).

In the book of James, just one sentence prior to the mention of Elijah being a man just like us, we read, "The effectual fervent prayer of a righteous man availeth much" (5:16).

In the very context that the Bible uses to proclaim, "These men were no different than you," we find that the issue at hand is prayer. Not just any kind of prayer, but "effectual fervent" prayer—prayer that works, prayer with fire, prayer with persistence, prayer with guts. For this kind of prayer, when offered via the means of a godly life, is guaranteed to change the world.

## Know What the Bible Says About Prayer

Before we go any further in this book, let's look at an overview of the Bible's promises regarding this sort of wrestling prayer—because this isn't merely the wild-eyed notion of Eric and Leslie Ludy, this is the revealed and unalterable opinion of Jesus Christ, Paul the apostle, James the brother of Jesus, the apostle Peter, the apostle John, and the rest of the great cloud of biblical writers. When you come to really understand what God says about praying, your faith and prayer muscles begin to flex.

Again and again in Scripture, Jesus says, "Ask, and it will be given to you."

Here's a quick sample:

> So I say to you, ask, and it will be given to you; seek, and you will find; knock, and it will be opened to you. For everyone who asks receives, and he who seeks finds, and to him who knocks it will be opened (Luke 11:9 NKJV).

While many of us have heard this promise, most of us don't actually believe it.

In another place, Jesus says, "If you ask anything in My name, I will do it."

Take a look:

> And whatever you ask in My name, that I will do, that the Father may be glorified in the Son. If you ask anything in My name, I will do it (John 14:12-13 NKJV).

*Anything*?

Come on! He couldn't mean that.

A lot of us even respond to the Bible, "I've tried that—it didn't work!"

Are we to believe we can ask for anything that comes to our mind and it will be given to us? How about a new Lexus? An acting career? A penthouse suite in downtown Manhattan?

To understand the mind of the Bible, every Scripture passage must pass through the "alignment test." In other words, it must be measured in light of every other scripture in the Bible. And lo and behold, there is another passage, found in the book of James, that helps us answer the Lexus question:

> You ask and do not receive, because you ask amiss, that you may spend it on your pleasures (James 4:3 NKJV).

Jesus says, "If you ask anything in My name, I will do it," but there are a couple biblical stipulations to this promise. First, as we just noted, you can't ask for selfish reasons—if you ask amiss, then *you will not receive*. And the second stipulation is found in the book of Matthew:

> Jesus answered and said to them, "Assuredly, I say to you, if you have faith and do not doubt...if you say to this mountain, 'Be removed and be cast into the sea,' it will be done. And whatever things you ask in prayer, believing, you will receive" (Matthew 21:21 NKJV).

Doubt is a prayer killer. Just as selfishness disables the effectiveness of prayer, so does unbelief. Jesus says, "Do not doubt." In other words, your faith must be unwavering, stouthearted, persistent, and immovable. It cannot be a hybrid of doubt and faith. It must be the pure-strain, the bold and daring request of the God-confident.

The promises of prayer are extraordinary, but for prayer to work as God promises it to work, it must be purged of self and doubt.

When David took the throne of Israel, one of the first things he ventured to do was to bring the Ark of Covenant to Jerusalem. Certainly this plan pleased God's heart. But God had prescribed a means of transporting the Ark, and unfortunately, David ignored this prescription. It was supposed to be carried only by the consecrated priests of God; no common man was ever supposed to touch it.

But a common man named Uzzah was assigned to help carry the sacred presence of God. He was a good man, but not a consecrated man from the lineage of Aaron. As the story goes, as the Ark was being carried, the oxen stumbled and Uzzah placed his hand on the side of the Ark to keep it from falling. Uzzah fell dead on the spot.

David felt in that moment the way many of us have felt in prayer. We genuinely desire to honor God, we have given ourselves to prayer with a sincere longing to interact with God. But, we have been like Uzzah. We have prayed as "common men," motivated by selfishness and encrusted with doubt, and have wondered why our prayers have hit the ceiling and fallen dead on the spot.

God cannot honor anything, no matter its degree of sincerity, if it is contrary to His Word.

David learned this truth through this experience, as I hope all of us do as well. And the next time he handled the sacred Ark, he did it according to the pattern of God. And guess what? It worked this time! God wanted that Ark in Jerusalem, but He couldn't violate His law, His pattern, His truth to accomplish His errands.

God has entrusted us, His children, with this nuclear "ark of prayer." He says, "I've given you the opportunity to shape history—to move mountains, calm storms, walk on water, and call fire down from heaven—but you must do it just as I would do it."

True prayer never violates the nature of God. What He is like is what our prayers should be like.

True prayer never asks for anything that Jesus wouldn't have asked for. What He asked is what we should be asking.

True prayer has the glory of God as its aim—not the comfort of men, nor the fleshly pleasures of humanity, but the fame and renown of Jesus Christ. This is the foremost intent of prayer.

And true prayer is confident in the power of prayer. It issues forth with assurance, knowing that when prayer is done in accordance with the pattern of God, in the nature of God, in alignment with the will of God, then it will be effective and it will be mightily answered.

True prayer must be offered out of a life that is true—true to God, true to Scripture, true in heart, true in motive, true in purity.

This is God's prescribed method for changing the world through prayer.

So, whether or not it would seem that the promises of Scripture regarding prayer seem a bit overblown, they will be realized only by those who are assured by their utter seriousness and their dead-on accuracy.

Look at a few of the choicest words on prayer in the New Testament. Read them closely, and let them sink in. For if what the Bible says about prayer is true, then the power of Moses, the confidence of Paul, and the heavenly persuasion of Elijah are ours for the taking.

And it would certainly behoove us to spend whatever time is necessary figuring out how to wield this nuclear weapon.

> This is the confidence that we have in him, that, if we ask any thing according to his will, he heareth us: and if we know that he hears us, whatsoever we ask, we know that we have the petitions that we desired of him (1 John 5:14-15).

> Most assuredly, I say to you, he who believes in Me, the works that I do he will do also; and greater works than these he will do, because I go to My Father. And whatever you ask in My name, that I will do, that the Father may be glorified in the Son. If you ask anything in My name, I will do it (John 14:12-13 NKJV).

> Again I say to you that if two of you agree on earth concerning anything that they ask, it will be done for them by My Father in heaven (Matthew 18:19 NKJV).

> Jesus said to him, "All things are possible to him who believes" (Mark 9:23 NKJV).

> Most assuredly, I say to you, whatever you ask the Father in My name He will give you. Until now you have asked nothing in My name. Ask, and you will receive, that your joy may be full (John 16:23-24 NKJV).

True prayer is not a selfish plea for comfort or blessing. It's a sacred communion with the Spirit of God, offered out of a life fully submitted to Him. And, as E.M. Bounds said, "Our praying needs to be pressed and pursued with an energy that never tires, a persistency which will not be denied, and a courage that never fails."[1]

Ask God to show you any faulty patterns in your prayer life. Do you pray merely for your comforts and desires? Do you ever pray when things are going well, or only when you are in dire need? Is your motive in prayer your own happiness, or the glory of God? Do you pray with an attitude of doubt, just going through the motions of prayer because it's the spiritual thing to do? Whatever problems God pinpoints within you, repent of your wrong attitudes and ask Him to remake and rebuild your approach to prayer.

If you find you are lacking in faith, ask Him for it! I love this statement from an "old divine," as quoted by E.M. Bounds:

> Would you be freed from the bondage to corruption? Would you grow in grace in general and grow in grace in particular? If you would, your way is plain. Ask of God more faith. Beg of him morning, and noon, and night, while you walk by the way, while you sit in the house, when you lie down and when you rise up; beg of him simply to impress divine things more deeply on your heart, to give you more and more of the substance of things hoped for and of the evidence of things not seen.[2]

# THE RUSH ON JEBUS
*the proving of loyalty and heart*

Joab—captain of the king's armed forces

❧ ERIC ❧

D avid was not just a man of valor, but a man of intimacy. His mighty men didn't just respect him and revere him—*they loved him*.

These men would gladly spend their blood for their king.

I can hear his mighty men say, "Just ask for our blood, precious leader, and it is yours!"

Even Saul's son, Jonathan, cared much about David. The Bible says, "The soul of Jonathan was knit with the soul of David, and Jonathan loved him as his own soul" (1 Samuel 18:1).

This man David was not just a heroic conqueror, but he was a heart-friend to the men in his persecuted band of devotees. He covenanted with them, saying his sword was their sword, his possessions their possessions, his name their name, his reputation their reputation, his strength their strength, his anointing their anointing, his kingdom their kingdom, and his swagger their swagger.

So is our Jesus more than just our strong champion and deliverer. He is also a heart-friend. He washed His mighty men's feet, He allowed His heroes to lean their heads upon His chest and feel the love of His noble heart beat for them. And He says to each of us, "Covenant with

Me, My son, My daughter! Let Me share with you all I have and all I am. I merely ask in return for all you have and all you are."

Like David, Jesus was a King who stirred the hearts of His followers with adoration and love. The Mighties of Christ were stripped naked and publicly beaten, they were stoned, they were sawn in pieces, they were crucified, they were fed to lions, and they were dipped in tar and burned alive to light Caesar's feasts. But these Mighties considered it their greatest pleasure to spend themselves for their beloved King.

*David* is a Hebrew name that simply means "beloved." He is the king that is dearly loved. He is the king men *want* to live for, fight for, and die for. It is not a duty to serve such a king; it is the greatest delight. It is not a sacrifice to suffer for such a king; it is the greatest privilege.

Such kings as David and Jesus breed followers born of the same heart. They inspire men to honor their name by becoming David-like and Christlike, by showcasing the same magnanimous nature.

Out of the soil of David's mighty nature grew heroic men like Joab, Jashobeam, Eleazar, Shammah, Abishai, and Benaiah. These men bore striking resemblance to their king, they had a single eye for his glory and his kingdom, and they walked the Judean countryside with their king's swagger and their king's regal nature in tow.

Out of the soil of Jesus' mighty nature grew such spiritual giants as Peter, Paul, John, James, Andrew, Stephen, and Philip. And like David's men, Jesus' Mighty Ones bore striking resemblance to their King. They had a single eye for His glory and His kingdom and they didn't just give themselves to His agenda; they gave up their lives to allow their King to live out His triumphant life in and through their bodies.

As Paul said, "It is no longer I who live but Christ lives in me" (Galatians 2:20 NASB).

Catch this secret: God's Gibborim are grown out of the soil of loving devotion to their King. They relinquish their lives and hand them over to their beloved Mighty Commander. This isn't how their journey on

Earth ends; rather, it's how their journey begins. Their dreams, their ambitions, their plans are given up for the dreams, ambitions, and plans of their Beloved. They sleep where He sleeps, they go where He goes, they love whomever He loves, and they hate whatever He hates. They belong, heart and soul, to their King, feeling what He feels, thinking what He thinks, saying what He says, serving whom He serves, and breaking the jaws of whatever evil beast He is set against.

And these men bear striking resemblance to their King as a result.

Let's consider one of the Mighties who stood loyally by David's side: Joab.

I would love to be like Joab.[1] He was King David's most trusted. He was chief and captain over David's entire army of men and one of David's three mightiest. Joab's example stirs me to the depths of my soul. He's manly; he's courageous; he's like his king.

Like David, Joab was born in Bethlehem (trust me, there is something in the water of this little town). He knew the heart of David, and he loved him with every fiber of his being. He covenanted with his heart-friend to stand for him, to defend his name, and was willing to spend his blood in whatever way necessary to see his king take what was rightfully his.

Joab stood with David through the season of persecution, and when the day finally came that David's kingdom came on earth as it was in heaven, Joab rose up to prove his love and loyalty to his commander.

Joab studied the heart-gaze of his precious leader and he saw it turn toward the castle of Zion. He saw the fire in his eyes, the anger kindle in his soul—this mighty fortressed city, also known as Jebus, was located right in the heart of David's land and yet it was ruled by the dark forces of the Jebusites. It mocked the power of God Almighty.

And Joab knew his king craved this castle as his very own.

Joab stayed close to his king's heart and waited for the moment, listening to his commander's pulse, monitoring his every thought, his every emotion.

And then the moment came, and Joab was ready.

David announced to all his Mighties, "He who draws first blood from the mocking faces of these evil Jebusites will win the position amongst my army and in my heart. The first to strike their smirking mouths will be chief and captain amongst my host!"

While David's vast army paused to consider such a proposal, Joab was already running. All alone ahead of the troupe, he ran, he climbed, he crushed the jaws of the enemy, braving the entire enemy host of the Jebusites. He ran at the very front, risking his blood to prove his soul's mettle, his soul's love to his leader. And it says in Scripture, "So Joab the son of Zeruiah went first up, and was chief" (1 Chronicles 11:6). That is, Joab was the first to go to Jerusalem and take it for his king.

When Jesus is crowned King within our souls, He turns His eyes longingly toward the city of Jebus within our inner lives. Are we following His gaze? Are we attuned to His heart the way Joab was attuned to David's? When David claimed Jebus, the castle of Zion, that fateful day so many thousands of years ago, he gave it a new name: *Jerusalem*.

Jesus too is after His Jerusalem.

The Mighties must be born in Bethlehem, but they must *grow up* unto Jerusalem.

Jerusalem is the holy place, the set-apart place. It's the place of the King's throne. It is the place of the temple of God, the place of redemption (the cross, the resurrection, the outpouring of God's very life), the place of sacrifice, the place of victory.

Jesus said, "I now must go up to Jerusalem."

Jesus was intimate with the heart of His Father in heaven. He knew His Father's gaze was upon that ancient city of David, and that the first one to strike the blow there would be the chief and captain of His Father's hosts. And like Joab, the mighty one of old, Jesus ran ahead of the armies of God, proving His great love and devotion—proving Himself not just a Mighty One, but the Most Mighty.

Jesus never asks us to risk, dare, or do anything that He Himself wouldn't do.

We read in Romans that Jesus was the firstborn among many brethren (8:29).

David is a historical and scriptural foreshadow of Jesus, but amazingly all of David's Mighties mentioned herein (Joab, Jashobeam, Shammah, Eleazar, Abishai, and Benaiah) also prove an incredible historical and scriptural foretaste of Jesus Christ. However, as men, what we see in these great heroes of the ancient past is intended to both introduce us to the glory of our great King Jesus as well as show us how we too can partake of this mighty nature.

This "Joab devotion" is a huge piece in the blueprint of the Mighty. And a critical piece in the machinery of wrestling prayer. For Jesus longs to acquaint you with His heart, to train you to follow His gaze, to anticipate His yearning, to know His every thought. Jesus longs to groom you as His Joab in order that you might be willing to be the first in this generation to "go up to Jerusalem" and suffer for your King's sake. He is looking for men who are moved by the same love He and David were moved by, men who do not count their lives as more valuable than the renown of their beloved God.

Remember, your King is not just heroic, He is an intimate heart-friend. And He longs to be an intimate heart-friend with you. He is not just majesty, He is mercy. He is not just power, He is personality. He is not just holy, He has a heart filled with love.

As mentioned earlier, we are in a season of persecution. Our King is in exile from this world. He wasn't welcomed when He was in the flesh on Earth and He still isn't welcomed today. His name is a byword and His reputation is soiled with ignorance and disdain. He is looking for His followers. He is looking for His Joabs, the men who are willing to stand with Him even when the times are dark and the hostility is great.

Don't discount the fact that God is calling you to be a Joab in this generation. God desires believers who are watchers of His heart, students of His thoughts, and followers of His gaze. He is longing for heart-friends.

There are many born in Bethlehem, but not every anointed one is willing to follow his or her rightful King into hiding and to share in His ignominy. But God's Gibborim follow, no matter the pain, no matter the cost to their reputation and their comfort. The Company of Heroes is moved not by duty but by love. May we become such men and women, and may we be moved by affection for our Beloved.

# *a moment for prayer*
## PRAYING GOD-PRAYERS

### ⤳ LESLIE ⤴

I'm going to share a very simple truth with you. In fact, it is so simple it's extremely easy to miss. So read it back over as many times as is necessary until you fully grasp this uncomplicated fact: God is the one who prays. All we must do is allow Him to pray His prayers in and through us.

Did you catch it?

Most of us think that prayer is an activity where we whip up a whole bunch of words and string them together in a spiritual-sounding fashion.

Prayer is not first and foremost talking to God, it's first and foremost listening to God.

Jesus said that the words He spoke were not His words, they were the words of His Father in heaven. Then He said that all the things He did were done because His Father was doing them (see John 14:10). As bewildering as this may seem, Jesus did nothing of His own accord. He did only that which His Father was doing.

That means that not only the living, moving, eating, drinking, preaching, healing, and teaching of Jesus were all a result of the Father's lead, but also the praying of Jesus. Jesus prayed only what the Father was praying.

Jesus did what the Father was doing, and our job as Christians is to do only what Jesus is doing. As Ian Thomas explained:

In spite of His eternal equality with the Father...the Lord
Jesus for our sakes made Himself *nothing* (Phil. 2:7), that
the Father might be everything and be glorified in Him! In
an attitude of total dependence, He exercised...that perfect
"faith-love" relationship for which we by Christ Himself have
been created![1]

The book of Hebrews says Jesus is our great High Priest (see 8:1-13).
Jesus is still laboring in intercessory prayer for us, for this world, and
for His purposes to be established in the Earth.

Jesus receives His prayers from the Father.

We receive our prayers from Jesus.

Jesus prays what the Father is praying.

We pray what Jesus is praying.

And thus, we are praying in concert with heaven and are assured
that if our prayers originate from God Himself, they will without a
doubt be answered.

## Do Jesus' Bidding

As Eric mentioned in the previous chapter, Joab had an eye for his
king. He lay his head close to him in the Cave of Adullam, intimately
acquainting himself with the longings, the lookings, and the purposes
of his king's heart. Therefore his errands were merely an enunciation
of that kingly heart. Such is our job in prayer.

Our job is as Joab's. Jesus is our King, but we are His lead captain within the territory of our soul. We do His bidding, we fight His
battles, and we only do that which our King is doing—we never go
off the reservation.

Whereas Joab ran errands on a physical battlefield, we run our
errands primarily on a spiritual plane. It's still a very real battle, but
it looks quite different.

Jesus is interested in sharing His prayers with us, just as David
was interested in sharing his strategies, his designs, and his will with
Joab.

But we must learn to listen. We must practice being still before our God and allow Him to speak. We must train our inner life to quiet itself and focus our attentions heavenward.

This is one of the most basic truths of the Christian life, and specifically of prayer. However, it is the easiest one to miss.

*God is the one who prays. All we must do is allow Him to pray His prayers in and through us.*

For some reason this simple principle rubs us the wrong way. We don't want to be limited to only the prayers of Jesus. We want to ask for things on our list, not just His list. We are afraid that if we pray only Jesus' prayers, our lives, needs, and desires will go overlooked.

Joab had to trust that when he put the interests of the king and the kingdom first, his king would tend to his personal needs.

As Jesus said, "Seek first the kingdom of God, and his righteousness; and all these [other things that you are concerned about] shall be added unto you" (Matthew 6:33).

So how does one gain such an intimate relationship with Jesus that he actually knows His prayers? Let's look at some practical ways to start:

### Spend Time with Your King

A.W. Tozer said, "The man who would know God must spend time with him."[2]

This is an issue of time. True prayer demands more of our life than most are willing to give. And therefore, few are those who ever taste of its power and delights.

But if you are serious about joining the Company of Heroes, and learning to pray the very prayers of Jesus, then you will need to begin to get radical with your daily schedule. You will need to make time for your King. Time to listen to Him, study Him, watch Him…and fall in love with Him.

Evaluate your sleep habits. Can they be changed to create more opportunity for prayer?

Evaluate your leisure activities. Can they be changed, or altogether abandoned, to create more room for intimate time with your Lord?

Evaluate your work schedule. Can it be altered to make prayer a greater priority? If not, can you find a different job, a new career?

Are there moments in your day that currently are being wasted on trivialities that could be transformed into something more sacred and eternal?

Most of us constantly battle with the fact that God seems distant, intimacy with Christ seems difficult to obtain, and our prayers don't seem to be heard. But God says, "You will seek Me and find Me, when you search for Me with all your heart" (Jeremiah 29:13 NKJV).

We aren't finding Him because we aren't searching for Him with *all our hearts*. We are too preoccupied with watching reality shows, too busy downloading the latest songs on iTunes, and too enamored with Hollywood's newest production to let our whole being be poured forth in constant and unreserved devotion in the service of the Lord who died to save us.

Most of us feel we don't have enough time for prayer and seeking God. But we don't even consider giving up our nightly TV time, our weekend movie fests, or our YouTube fetish in exchange for spending time in His presence.

First Timothy 5:6 says that those who live in pleasure are dead while they live. Are we living for pleasure, or living for Him?

When we began to get serious about wrestling prayer, Eric and I made a decision to break our addiction to worldly entertainment and instead use our downtime for prayer. I know at first glance that kind of decision sounds bleak and miserable. But ironically, it's been the other way around. This step of obedience has led to the most exhilarating season in life we have ever known. Our relationships with Jesus are more real and intimate than they have ever been. His Word has become more powerful and living to us than ever before. Prayer is being heard and miraculously answered like never before. Spending an hour in the presence of God is more refreshing and renewing to me than any Hollywood "mind escape" could ever be.

Of course, this was not an easy step to take. Our sinful, selfish natures screamed and kicked in disapproval in the beginning. Prayer seemed laborious, and we longed for something to coddle our flesh. As I said in my book *Set-Apart Femininity*, we even tried to watch Disney movies with our two-year-old son as a way of "escaping and relaxing." But just about the time we decided to yield our entertainment fetish as an offering to our Lord, our little boy decided—completely on his own—that he no longer enjoyed movies. Whenever we tried to turn on *Mary Poppins* or *Herbie*, he would frown and say, "Turn it off pwease!" (God seemed to be helping us along in breaking our entertainment fetish.)

Every human rationale presented itself, trying to convince us that such a decision was completely unnecessary and that our relationship with Christ would be just as vibrant if we spent our night in front of *Pirates of the Caribbean* as if we spent our night in front of His throne.

But now we know better. When we become dead to the world and dead to our flesh, we become alive in Christ, and He becomes alive in us. Here is how I explained this transformation in my book *Set-Apart Femininity*:

> The question, "Would you rather watch a movie tonight, or spend some time in prayer?" used to make me laugh. It wasn't even a contest—the movie option *always* won out. I mean, why would I deliberately choose to give up pleasure and fun in exchange for dullness and drudgery? But that was before I really *experienced* that "in His presence is fullness of joy and in His right hand are pleasures forevermore." The pleasure and delight I have discovered in the presence of God have far surpassed any fleeting enjoyment I used to gain from the worldly counterfeit version.
>
> It is something that can only be understood when experienced. I have far greater joy, peace, and heavenly perspective in my daily life. I am far less encumbered by mental distractions and worldly preoccupations. The "self" part of me is

not being stroked and coddled and, therefore, I have greater victory over sin on a daily basis. The rest and refreshment He brings is so fulfilling that my controlling need for "down time" in front of movies has completely vanished. A powerful prayer session gives me all the peace, strength, and renewal I could ever want or need. It's truly supernatural. I have no desire to return to where I was before, escaping reality and vicariously living out fake adventures on the big screen. I am far too caught up in the real-life adventure of the set-apart, Christ-infused life. And the real thing is *so* much better than the counterfeit.[3]

If you want an earth-shattering prayer life, be willing to do whatever it takes. No matter how much your flesh may scream in protest, seek Jesus Christ with all your heart. When you do, I can guarantee you will not be disappointed.

# THE COMPANY OF HEROES
*the sacred list of the valiant*

ERIC

The biblical record is astounding. And it is awe-inspiring to realize that we have the privilege of entering into intimate communion with the very God who directed the formation of that ancient 66-book volume.

The men in this grand book performed exploits and wrought wonders that shook the world in their day. These men knew the power and grandeur of their God.

Do *we* know the power and grandeur of our God in our day? Does our generation comprehend that the God of the Bible is without "shadow of turning" and that He is "the same yesterday, today, and for ever"?[1]

It seems to me that we spend most of our spiritual energies trying to explain why the God of Elijah, Samson, David, and Paul seems to have lost His muscle in our modern age. Did He grow tired of performing heroics? Did He wax feeble after all these years of running this whole universal show?

Could it be true that God has really lost His muscle? Maybe it would be more accurate to say *God lost His men*.

Leslie talked about Elijah earlier in this book, and I think he is worth a repeat visit. Here is a guy who called down fire from heaven and slew 450 priests of Baal. In his elder years he outran the chariot of Ahab, and prayed such that the sky ceased to give rain to Israel for three-and-a-half years.

It begs the question: Is this guy even human?

Once again, that's why James goes out of his way to make clear that "Elijah was a man with a nature like ours" (James 5:17 NKJV). He was just as human as you and me, and yet he possessed something greater than what we have in our softy rendition of Christianity in this modern era. But let me say this: What Elijah possessed is not something greater than what Christ promises us we too can have.

Samson grabbed ahold of the gates of Gaza and carried them off (Judges 16:3). The gates of a city! He just ripped these dudes off their hinges and toted them away. He took the jawbone of a donkey and killed 1000 Philistines with it (15:14-15). *A thousand men all by himself!*

Elijah and Samson were real-life men, empowered and enabled by the Spirit of Almighty God. And just as they were strengthened for the real-life battles of their day, we are made mighty for the real-life battles of our day. Our battles may not demand the outrunning of chariots and the carrying away of city gates, but they still do demand a supernatural enablement.

And yet there is a vast shortage of believers who simply believe with childlike faith that God even desires to build such superheroes in our modern day. We have far more faith in the power of the enemy to defeat us than we do in the power of our God to deliver us, change us, empower us, and demonstrate His mighty nature in and through us.

I, for one, believe. And I am throwing my hat in the ring, pushing all my chips onto the table. I refuse to have a form of godliness that denies the power thereof. I want the real thing, not some trumped-up show of emotion, not some Christian light show, not some sugarcoated sermon about God loving me still even though I am covered in filth and once again trounced under the feet of my enemies. I want the ancient power that coursed through the veins of Joshua, the ancient strength that stirred within the soul of Gideon, the ancient passion that overcame Josiah, and the ancient courage that gushed forth from the soul of Daniel.

I don't know about you, but I refuse to accept our modern rendition of Christian mediocrity as God's best for His church. I refuse to accept this paltry show of human love, this pitiful wheeze of hope, and this candy-coated defeat as the real thing.

I read the Bible and my soul is stirred. I see men who stood alone in their age, crying for the people of God to once again return to the real thing. I see women who gave themselves as broken bread and poured out wine for their beloved King, believers who had a substance, a fire, a power, a courage, and a love wholly different than that which is showcased today by our modern troubadours of the gospel.

And this is why my soul burns for the Order of the Mighties, the Company of Heroes, God's Gibborim to once again arise. Countless millions of so-called Christians are frittering their lives away in a powerless, defeated, miserable wilderness of half-doubts, sinful bondage, and paralyzing fears. They have God, but they only have the crumbs of His person. They have life, but it's a life upon a hospital bed, intravenously being maintained by selfish consumption and fleshly addictions.

I refuse this hollow form of life and godliness. I yearn for something more, something better, something real.

For me, I long to be included on Christ's list. I long to have a name among the Mighties. I esteem this as the most worthwhile use of my life on this Earth. I have forsaken all for my King's kingdom and His glory. And in so doing, I have found the God of the Bible taking form within my soul. That ancient strength, that ancient power, that ancient passion, and that ancient courage are beginning to emblazon themselves upon my inner man.

For years of my life I have opened up to 1 Chronicles chapter 11 and 2 Samuel 23 and salivated. There is something so utterly manly contained within those chapters and it thumps upon my chest and calls forth something gritty and growling within me.

Just listen to the grand story, the sacred tribute to David's Mighties. It's almost as if God were bragging about His boys:

There was Joab, who was commander over all of David's forces—he was the first to rush upon Jebus and strike the mocking grins off the faces of the Jebusites and reclaim his king's honor. He was numbered among the three mightiest and was David's closest confidante.

There was Jashobeam (the Tachmonite), who was chief among David's 37 Mighties. He too was numbered among the three mightiest. He lifted up his spear against 800, whom he slew at one time.

There was Eleazar, who, along with Joab and Jashobeam, rounded out the hallowed troupe of the three mightiest under David. It says of him that when all Israel fled before the Philistines, and a parcel of land at Pasdammim was left exposed to the enemy, he stood his ground, along with his king, and smote the Philistines until his hand was weary. But even in his weakness his hand burned unto the hilt of his sword and he kept swinging. We read that "the LORD wrought a great victory that day" (2 Samuel 23:10).

There was Shammah, who though he didn't rank among the first three Mighties, was named amongst the second three. He too, along with Eleazar, stood with his king in Pasdammim, standing in the midst of the sacred parcel of ground yielding not an inch unto the enemies of his beloved king. When all others fled, and it appeared that defeat was imminent, Shammah would not turn from the side of his commander. And as a result, the Philistines were devastated and the victory was supernaturally achieved.

There was Abishai, the brother of Joab. As Joab commanded the first three Mighties, so Abishai was commissioned the chief of the second three Mighties. It says of Abishai that he lifted up his spear against 300 and slew them. He is credited in 2 Samuel 21 with killing one of the four sons of Goliath and, in doing so, rescuing King David's life. He followed his king into the heart of Saul's camp while Saul's army slept, and with a spiritual swagger reminiscent of his commander, he grabbed Saul's spear and a cruse of water from Saul's intimate satchel and carried them away in the night (1 Samuel 26:11-12).

Then there was Benaiah, who, along with Shammah and Abishai, rounded out the illustrious second tier of David's Mighties. He was assigned to be captain of the king's bodyguard, for he was a man of extraordinary valor. Scripture says of Benaiah that he did "many acts."

In fact, his résumé sounds quite similar to his king's—he slew two lionlike men of Moab. In a time of snow, he went down into a pit and slew a lion. He slew a giantlike Egyptian warrior by stripping him of his own massive spear and killing him with his own weapon.

This list of Mighties is extraordinary! It is bigger-than-life heroism on display in the annals of history!

The list goes on to include the 30 captains over David's armies. Asahel, another brother of Joab, was named among these 30 captains. We read of Asahel that he "was as fleet of foot as a wild gazelle."[2]

There was Elhanan, who stood against the giant brother of Goliath and roundly defeated him.[3]

There was Jonathan who with a Davidic swagger slew the six-fingered, six-toed giant of Gath who dared to defy Israel.[4]

And in addition to Jonathan were Shammah, Elika, Helez, Ira, Abiezer, Mebunnai, Zalmon, and Maharai—all mighty men, men of renown, men of great valor in their generation.

There were Heleb, Ittai, Benaiah, Hiddai, Abialbon, and Azmaveth—all captains in this courageous Company of Heroes, brave to stand with their king in life and share with their king in death.

There were Eliahba, Shammah, Ahiam, Eliphelet, Eliam, and Hezrai—men made great and powerful warriors by the love and inspiration of their commander and chief.

And there were Paarai, Igal, Bani, Zelek, Naharai, Ira, Gareb, and Uriah—God's Gibborim, God's hand-selected men chosen to champion the cause of David's kingdom, David's throne, and David's glory.

We read in 1 Chronicles 11 that these men were men of might and men of war, fit for the battle. They could handle shield and buckler. Their faces were like the faces of lions, and they were as swift as the roes upon the mountains.

Would you blame me for saying that it is my great desire to travel back in time and be amongst such mighty men? Would you blame me for longing to be included upon such a list in the kingdom of my Jesus?

We read in Scripture, there were "thirty and seven in all" (2 Samuel 23:39).

*Thirty-seven.*

There were only 37 spots on the list. Or, you could say, only 37 men were worthy of being included on such a sacred list. David's armies numbered in the hundreds of thousands, and yet only 37 men made "the list."[5]

What did these 37 men choose to do in their strength? They chose to leave all and stand to confirm David as king.

I believe every generation has a list. I'm sure the scribes of heaven chronicle the great events of Earth and they notate the King's list in every generation. Won't it be a thrill to read the lists of the ages when the kingdom comes?

Will you and I be on the list for this generation? Will our King call out our name as one of His Mighties, or will we merely be numbered amongst the multitudes of those who merely believed the basics?

I long to be one of Christ's closest confidantes. And I long for you to join me in such a pursuit. For even if I am not privileged to make the list, it would be my greatest pleasure to see your name there. I long to be there with you, but my life would be well spent even if I didn't crack the 37, if it inspired you to rise to such a lofty position in the kingdom of our great and precious Leader.

But I must warn you, I plan on presenting you with some very stiff competition. I will not surrender to mediocrity and I will not allow my life to be numbered amongst the multitudes if I have a choice in the matter.

My encouragement to you is to yearn for the prized position of Joab. Set your sights to the position of the apostle John, of whom it says that he was the one "whom Jesus loved" (John 13:23). Seek to know your King in such a way—to lean your head upon His chest, to know His most intimate thoughts. For this is where the Mighties are made.

They are not made in seminaries, they are not made in Bible colleges, they are not made in missionary training programs. Rather, they are made in the secret place of communion, the sacred closet of prayer.

We live in a generation where young Christians are not encouraged to seek to be named amongst the dearest 37. We don't even realize that our King is hiding in Ziklag and is yearning for eager young heroes to surround Him in His hiding, to share in His sufferings, and to know the power of His resurrection. Jesus is beckoning an entirely new generation of Mighties to surround Him, to know Him, to love Him, to fight for Him, to die for Him, and to perform the most stunning exploits for all the world to behold.

# a moment for prayer
## The Travailing Prevailers

⊰ Leslie ⊱

Our world applauds its Olympians. Those hearty men and women who dedicate themselves to the flag of their homeland, suffer the hardships of years of vigorous training, and accept the loss of certain fleshly privileges and comforts for a season in order to bring back the gold for their country.

But Olympians, with all their earthly shimmer and human glory, pale next to the list of God's Mighties. To pole vault, to sprint 200 meters, to throw a javelin, to nail a floor exercise, or to win eight gold medals single-handedly are paltry uses of the human body—a body designed to house the Fire and Living Presence of the Most High God.

Through our earthly lens we can see the luster of these Olympic heroes, but we often don't comprehend the heavenly luster of God's Wrestlers, God's Intercessors, God's Gibborim.

It's the men and women who pray who earn God's standing ovation and receive the awesome shower of heaven's anthem. These are the Mighty, these are the ones doing the trench digging, the pipe laying, the jackhammering in the city of their God. God builds His church upon the shoulders of these blue collar Mighties. In fact, He says that the world is not even worthy of them (see Hebrews 11:38).

An Olympian is asked to endure a starvation of certain fleshly pleasures for a season in order to gain earthly glory and fame. But God's

Company of Heroes are asked to forgo a "normal" life on this Earth, to give up the good opinion of the masses, to carry in their very bodies the sufferings of their Lord, and accept the fact that they will be considered the offscouring of this world.

But whereas God's Gibborim don't possess anything here on Earth, they do possess untold riches in heaven. They share in the intimate fellowship of their King and become His means of changing this world, saving souls, and rescuing the weak.

An Olympian seeks to prevail because he or she is attempting to win a victory that is not yet gained. But God's Heroes seek to *travail* and to prevail—to bring about a victory that has already been achieved by Jesus Christ.

Many of us have never seen the sort of prayer that the apostle Paul refers to as "travail of the soul" (John 16:21; Galatians 4:19; 1 Thessalonians 2:9; 2 Thessalonians 3:8). The visual picture given is one of a woman giving birth to a child. In other words, the life is there, it just needs to be brought forth. This sort of prayer is painful, hot with tension, and motivated by ardent devotion.

## Learning to Travail

The labor and delivery of my firstborn, Hudson, was 39 hours of agony. I received no painkillers, I went through it au naturel. It was difficult. There were moments I was sure I was going to die. It was travail. I wasn't feeling pain because it was enriching to my soul; I was in agony for a real life, for a real promise to come forth into this world.

This is the very picture that Paul chooses to utilize in order to describe prayer.

There is something that God wants to be born in this world. But this "something" is unable to come forth without a fight, without some serious contractions, and without someone willing to do the pushing.

God's Mighties are those who stand up and say, "God, I'm willing to feel the pain of the necessary contractions—I'm willing to travail."

The Bible says Jesus sweat great drops of blood not just upon the cross, but in prayer. Jesus said to His Father, "Not my will, but thine!" He travailed; He took on the fight; He felt the most severe pain; and He did the agonizing work that none of us were equipped to do.

We read of the Scottish minister John Welch that he often soaked his pillow with tears during prayer, being in agony over the lost and the great travesty of God's glory being diminished in the streets of culture. John Welch said before he died that he counted a day ill spent if he did not put seven or eight hours into secret prayer.

David Livingstone, the famous African explorer-missionary, lived in prayer and literally died upon his knees in prayer. The often-repeated cry echoing from his soul was, "When will the wounds of this world's sin be healed?"[1]

David Brainerd, the cowhide-clad missionary to the American Indians, inspired some of the greatest men of our day and age in their prayer life. He gave himself to wrestling prayer, and died at the age of 29. I believe (along with others who have studied his life) that Brainerd accomplished more spiritually in those years than the majority of our modern Christian leaders have over the past 20.

Rees Howells literally spent years in prayer, wrestling to see a specific heavenly burden born into this earthly reality. His prayer life is second to none in his fight, his persistence, and his vigor—he would simply not let go until the life was born. For one stretch of 11 months he prayed 11 hours a day for the money to purchase a Bible college in England. This man saw mighty revivals in Africa come forth from prayer, multitudes healed from incurable diseases, and evil earthly empires during World War II literally foiled in their military advance due to the wrestling hold of intercession.

John "Praying" Hyde, the mighty missionary to India, prayed for weeks on end without letting go of his position in prayer. So passionate was Hyde for lost souls that he physically carried a contorting agony for these lost ones, weeping, writhing with the contractions of spirit to see these heathens enter the kingdom of heaven.

Evan Roberts spent years in a prayer closet from his mid-teens until his mid-twenties, pleading for revival in Wales. His cry was, "Lord,

bend me!" The subsequent outpouring of the Spirit of God upon
Wales proved one of the most extraordinary testimonies of the power
of prayer this world has ever seen. The effects of the Welsh revival
shook the entire world.

George Muller demonstrated to an entire generation of Christians
that God is a prayer-answering God. Without ever bringing financial
needs before the public, he sought to prove that by confiding only to
God his needs—through the power of wrestling prayer—a man can
live, thrive, and change this world for Jesus Christ. His life, like all
the others mentioned above, was replete with miracle after miracle. It
is said of Muller that he raised over 1000 orphans, fed them, clothed
them, and educated them on the power of prayer.

George Whitefield, the mighty man of God who stormed early
America with the gospel and was a critical role player in the First Great
Awakening, acknowledged that he would spend whole days and weeks
prostrate on the ground in silent or vocal prayer.

Like the Heroes listed in Hebrews 11, this list of Mighty Heroes
could go on and on: William Carey, Edward Payson, Robert Murray
McCheyne—all were giants in the realm of prayer, and all were in
concert with McCheyne's belief that prayer was in fact, the "greatest
of all human offices that the soul of man can exercise."[2]

This is not to mention Amy Carmichael, Madame Guyon, Count
Zinzendorf, John Fletcher, John Knox, and the giant of prayer after
whom we named our firstborn son, Hudson Taylor.

Or how about Leonard Ravenhill, William Booth, John Wesley,
Andrew Murray, R.A. Torrey, E.M. Bounds, or the God-fearing Henry
Martyn, who pronounced, "Let me burn out for God. After all, whatever God may appoint, prayer is the great thing. Oh, that I may be a
man of prayer!"[3]

This is God's list of Gibborim. Each of these people spent their lives
on their knees, with Olympic-like givenness, and competed for crowns
that were not of this Earth. Each of these were so much more than
human athletes, human scholars, human philosophers, humanitarians,
and human celebrities—they were men and women who ensured the

glory of God in their generation, who fought to see truth victorious, who held back the tide of evil for yet another season.

There has been a movement afoot in the past 40 years in the church to diminish the example that these prayer-heroes have set for us to follow. Ever so subtly the idea that what these men and women did with their lives was "extreme" and "unnecessary," and therefore unmerited to mimic and find inspiration in today, has crept into the modern church's thinking.

But if there was ever a time for us to go to extremes for our God, it is now. The truth of the gospel is being diluted, dumbed down, and trampled upon by the very ones entrusted to keep it sacred and whole. It may seem "unnecessary" to get on your knees for multiple hours each and every day, but, may I remind you that unless someone rises up and says, "Lord, I'm willing to travail," there are lives, promises, and spiritual realities that will not be born into our day and age.

Effectual, fervent prayer is how God changes this world and bestows upon it the beauty, grace, and power that He purchased at the cross.

These men and women were not in the least bit extreme. They were merely Christians. If you need a little inspiration in the art of spiritual travail, study the lives of these great heroes of the faith. Ask God to teach and train you from their examples. Ask Him to make you worthy of the calling you have received. And tune out every voice that says you aren't equipped for this kind of praying. God has appointed you and me for this sacred task. Who will become the George Whitefields, the Hudson Taylors, and the John Welches of this generation if we do not answer the call?

# THE 800 DEAD

*the strength of love*

Jashobeam—chief over the king's
captains and one of the three mightiest

⊰ ERIC ⊱

My two-year-old son, Hudson, came up to me yesterday, tugged on my sleeve, and smiled grandly. His big brown eyes blinked up at me with little-boy excitement.

"Guess what?" he stated with bubbling enthusiasm.

"What?" I answered back playfully.

"I have a nickname for you, Daddy!" he pronounced.

Well, I didn't even know that he knew what a nickname was, let alone that he could muster up the mental acumen to invent one for me.

With great fascination I said, "What is it?"

"Da-doe!" he exclaimed with great pride.

I repeated my newfound nickname back to myself and cherished it with great affection as it rolled off my tongue.

"Da-doe! I really like it!"

Then I asked Hudson what *his* nickname was. He thought for a second and then proclaimed with an energetic shout, "Bee-doe!"

Nicknames are a symbol of affection. They are a statement of endearment, a token of close friendship. I have more than 20 nicknames for Hudson. Some I use more regularly than others, but all of them, when spoken, are enunciations of my rich fatherly love for my precious boy. And if I were to share these nicknames with you they would merely strike you as strange because you weren't there at their inception—you missed the beautiful father-son moments in which they originated.

For instance, I call my son "B," and it's a long story to try and explain it. He also is my "Lump of Love," "My Bundle of Big Time," my "Shorn Bjorn," my "Bundleloupe" (which means he's half Bundle of Big Time and half Cantaloupe), "Gene Longbody," "Bobs Longfellow," "Shnug-a-lug," and my "Big Pile of Good Mood." To attempt to explain these names only seems to detract from their inherent mysterious nature, which is wrapped up in the beautiful love story that the two of us (father and son) share day in and day out.

My son's official name may be Hudson Jack Ludy. But official names are for legal documents and business dealings. Nicknames are for life, for love, for intimacy, and for expressions of heart affection.

This may sound strange, but Jesus has nicknames for all of His children. He knows our official names, but He isn't bound by formalities; rather, He is moved by intimacy.

To one of His three mightiest, whom we know historically as Peter, but whose official name was Simon, Jesus said, "You are 'My Rock'!"

Jesus nicknamed Simon "My Rock!" He called him *Petros* (Peter). He basically was saying, "You are a soul unyielding!"

To one of His other three mightiest, named John, Jesus said, "You are 'The One I Love'!"

Where there is affection, there are nicknames. Where there is love, everything official melts away.

David had an army of hundreds of thousands of men, and yet out of all those men Jashobeam was known intimately by his king. He was the chief of David's captains, as well as one of the king's three mightiest. He held a significant place in the political and military landscape of Israel, and yet even for his high position and growling masculine presence, his king referred to him by a nickname: "Adino the Eznite" (2 Samuel 23:8).

Isn't it somewhat odd to think that David's Mighties had nicknames?

When we think of soldiers we think of valor, strength, grit, and gusto, so it's a bit jarring to realize these men were precious to their king. They had a deep, warm, personal connection with the powerful anointed ruler of Israel. In fact, these men were so precious to their king that he called them by nicknames.

Adino the Eznite?

I realize this might not sound like the most flattering nickname, but to Jashobeam this name represented the living, breathing love of his king. It reminded him that he was affectionately loved and appreciated. He was cherished as an individual man and not merely as a warrior for the kingdom.

In our English vernacular, the nickname Adino the Eznite doesn't quite have the ring of poetry and beauty that many of us prefer. It sounds rather cartoonish and awkward. But in the Hebrew it was anything but. It was something that sort of sounded like *'Etsen 'Adiynow*. But it wasn't the sound of the name that evoked such deep affection between David and Jashobeam, it was the meaning behind the name.

David would proclaim, "You are *'Etsen 'Adiynow!*" and a hush would fall over the entire host of Israel, for such a name was sacred, it was honor in its highest form. It was a name earned through stripes, through victory in battle. It was a name above other names in that it spoke of proven valor, courage, fortitude, and triumph.

Israel maybe more than any nation on Earth can appreciate such a nickname as *'Etsen 'Adiynow*. For the name *Israel* itself was an affectionate nickname given to Jacob after he wrestled through the night with God and prevailed. It was a name of great warmth and heroism. And it became the name of God's people. It was as if God were saying, "My precious people are 'the Prevailers,' 'the Mighty Conquerors,' 'the Overcomers.'"

*'Etsen 'Adiynow*.

The Hebrew words packaged in this nickname are not typical, and therefore have proven challenging for scholars to fully pin down. But there are certain beautiful attributes of this name that speak volumes.

The word *'Etsen* seems to denote a weapon of God, sharp to the dividing of joint and marrow, and strong to the destruction of darkness.

And the word *'Adiynow* seems to create a picture of a king's glory, a king's crown, a king's badge of the triumph. It's like the reward given by a king after victory, such as an ornament about a victor's neck.

And when these words coalesce into one name, they become something even more powerful and demonstrative. They seem to become more than a name, they become a story. They shout the tale of a mighty man, hot and ardent with the flame of fiery love, lifting up a sharp, strong weapon, destroying the host of darkness, and proving the glory of his beloved king.

*'Etsen 'Adiynow* is no mere name. It is a name above other names. It is a name that boasts of triumph and boasts of indefatigable strength. It proclaims that the impossible has been accomplished. It says that one man has stood against 800 and vanquished every last one to preserve his beloved king's throne.

Jashobeam comes in from the battle, his body trembling with fatigue, his hands, his face, his spear covered in the blood of his enemies and he kneels before the throne of his king.

"For your glory," he whispers, bowing his head in worship, his hand still clinging to his spear.

David is moved with love and affection as he looks upon Jashobeam. The king gazes upon this man with tears of warmth and endearment flowing freely down his cheeks. This man did not just preserve Israel, but he touched and deeply moved the heart of his beloved commander.

And as it says in Chronicles, "The name was *'Etsen 'Adiynow.*"

It is such moments that beg a new name, a higher name, a better name be given. And the king is more than happy to oblige.

Do you realize that Jashobeam was merely a foretaste of the heroism of Jesus Christ? Jesus was the mighty man, hot and ardent with the flame of fiery love, lifting up a sharp, strong weapon, destroying the host of darkness, and proving the glory of His beloved Father in heaven.

He was and is *'Etsen 'Adiynow.* He was the one given the name
above all other names. He was the weapon of God, sharp and strong,
plunged into the heart of darkness. Jashobeam used a physical sword
to vanquish his physical enemies, but Jesus Himself was the sharp,
strong sword known as the Word of God, a sword that devastated
every last power of hell and darkness.

Jesus was the glory of God made manifest, He was the victory of
God made flesh, and He was the precious ornament of triumph placed
about the neck of the Father.

What tenderness the Father has in His eyes as He looks upon His
victorious Son. What a smile must fill His heart, what tears must
stream His cheeks.

I love this statement about Jesus in Revelation 19:

> And I saw heaven opened, and behold a white horse; and he
> that sat upon him was called Faithful and True, and in righ-
> teousness he doth judge and make war. His eyes were as a
> flame of fire, and on his head were many crowns; and *he had
> a name written [on Him], that no man knew, but he himself.*
> And he was clothed with a vesture dipped in blood: and his
> name is called The Word of God (verses 11-13).

Now I italicized that line because I want you to ponder it. Jesus
has a name written on Him that none of us know. His Father has
given Him a name that is so intimate, so beautiful, so precious that
we as men are not yet able to know it. We know that His name is
*the Word of God.* We know that He is called *Faithful and True.* And
even later in this scriptural sequence we also know that on His thigh
is inscribed the name *King of kings and Lord of lords.* However, there
is yet a name that we don't yet know. And it is something even better
than *'Etsen 'Adiynow.* It is the name given Him in the secret place of
fellowship with His Father.

I'm going to hearken back to something I emphasized in chapter 6
when I talked of the intimate connection God holds with His Mighties. To our God, this life and battle on planet Earth is personal. This

isn't just some business transaction of soul, where He desires us to "sign our name here" and then He transfers into our name the right to be called one of His children. This is not some distant process accomplished through the power of attorney. Jesus, just like David, lives amidst His men. He doesn't rule them from a distance, He stands with them in battle, fights next to them, sleeps beside them, and shares both their joys and their griefs. He is called Immanuel—*God with us.*

In other words, He's a nickname-giver. He is touched by the words, affections, obedience, and heroic actions of His Mighties, and He isn't slow to give them names of endearment or honor.

Jashobeam is such a beautiful picture of Jesus Christ. We read in 1 Corinthians 1:24 that Christ is "the wisdom of God." In other words, He is the mind, the attitude, the perfect thinking pattern of the Almighty. In 1 Chronicles 11 and in 2 Samuel 23 we read of Jashobeam that he is the son of wisdom. The words in the Hebrew are *Tachmonite* or *Hachmonite,* but both words denote the same idea of wisdom. This man gained the name *'Etsen 'Adiynow* because he was fashioned in his mind after the thinking patterns of his king, after the thinking patterns of God.

Let me ask you a question.

Does it sound like "wisdom" to take on 800 venomous warriors single-handedly?

In our world, this sounds like stupidity.

But let's think about Jesus.

Does it sound like wisdom to come to Earth in the form of a fragile baby, born seemingly illegitimately to a teenage girl, in an obscure little town, wholly unrecognized as God except by some lowly shepherds and some foreign wise men? Does it sound like wisdom to turn yourself over to the evil powers of this Earth and subject yourself to torture and crucifixion, receive public mockery, and not even open your mouth to defend yourself?

Again, if we weren't so used to the bizarre story, we would have to admit this sounds a bit like lunacy.

But, whether it matches with our perception of wisdom or not, this is what God goes out of His way to define as "His version" of wisdom. It's a wisdom that is higher than the wisdom of man.

God's Mighties must be shaped by His kind of wisdom. We must adopt His mind in all matters.

The Gibborim of God are men and women who allow the *'Etsen 'Adiynow,* the sharp and strong Weapon of God, Jesus Christ, to rise up within their inner lives, with the hot and ardent flame of fiery love, and utterly devastate the host of darkness within their souls. They are men and women who are proven by the Word of God, men and women who tremble before God's opinion, and men and women who thus prove the glory of their beloved King.

Jesus is *'Etsen 'Adiynow.* He is the Wisdom of God, the Weapon of God, the Word of God. And, like Jashobeam, he is the Chief of the Captains of the Mighty Host. As the Word of God He inspects, proves, and trains His heroes according to His perfect standard. And He utterly defeats every last enemy in our inner lives so that He may set us free to perform His mighty exploits. For He longs to say to us, "Thou art *'Etsen 'Adiynow.*"

Our King chooses for His Mighties both names that are public and names that are not for anyone else to know.

Would you long for a name of affection, given you by the Most High?

If so, then partake of His wisdom. Allow the Word of God to enter into the weedy forest of your soul and remove every last thing that stands against His kingdom purpose in your life. Let Him destroy the 800 Philistines within your heart and mind. Let him pull down every thought that esteems itself higher and truer than the Word of God itself.

Are you proud?

Let His Word humble you, break you, expose your weakness, your need, and your desperation.

Are you polluted?

Let His Word inspect you and try you against the perfection of

Jesus Christ. Let Him sting your soul with His sword of truth in order that He may uproot the iniquity and replace it with His purity.

Are you cowardly?

Let His Word inspire in your soul the wisdom of Jashobeam, the heroism of Joab, the spiritual swagger of David. Let Him train you that whenever you stand up for your King, no matter how idiotic it might seem to the world, it is esteemed higher than anything else in heaven. Let His Word charge you to grab the mane of the lion, the neck of the bear, the sword out of Goliath's hand—let it teach you to walk straight into the den of darkness and rip the souls of the lost right out of Lucifer's hands.

I want to be Eric the Tachmonite (the wise). I want to be my King's *'Etsen 'Adiynow.* I want His sharp strong weapon to be so much a part of my soul that I live and breathe it. I want to stand when every other Israelite turns and runs. I want to kneel in the presence of my King, splattered in the demon-blood of the powers of the dark realm and whisper, "For your glory, my King!"

God isn't looking for Christians who are born after the wisdom of this world. He doesn't need "cautious" or "careful" men and women who, under the banner of wisdom, let the lions run off with the precious sheep of God, who allow bears to outrage and diminish the glory of the King of Israel, or who allow the Goliaths to stand and openly mock the armies of the living God unmolested.

He is looking for believers patterned after David, after Jesus, after the one called *'Etsen 'Adiynow.* He wants men and women who are unafraid of death, unashamed of truth, unabashed about hanging naked on a cross before a multitude of mocking onlookers. He wants followers who are seemingly careless, reckless in the fight of their King, seemingly presumptuous in the battle for the sheep of God, and seemingly lunatic in their willingness to tackle the enemy hosts all by their lonesome.

He wants warriors undaunted by the hosts of 10,000. He wants heroes fully awakened to the realities of their King's cause, love, and glory. He wants men and women who refuse to allow darkness to reign in their hearts and minds. He wants men and women who are willing to rise up with the hot and ardent flame of fiery love and utterly devastate the host of darkness within their own souls and in the souls of others about them.

Jashobeam shared a common mind with his king.

Do you?

Ephesians 5:3 says, "Fornication, and all uncleanness, or covetousness, let it not be once named among you, as becometh saints."

What is named among us that doesn't befit the sacred calling upon our lives?

In Galatians chapter 5, we read that those who practice immorality, impurity, sensuality, idolatry, sorcery, enmities, strife, jealousy, outbursts of anger, disputes, dissensions, factions, envying, drunkenness, carousing, and things like these will not inherit the kingdom of God.

If such practices are resident within our lives, then, dear God, we must allow the sharp strong edge of *'Etsen 'Adiynow* to set us free, deliver us, and wholly alter our existence.

In 2 Timothy 3, the apostle Paul clarifies the spiritual filth that must be purged from the soul of the Mighties. God's Gibborim cannot be hampered by such things. Paul's list digs deep, it cuts, it exposes all that is diminishing Christianity in our modern age. But, as much as the contents of this list may sting the soul with conviction, it's merely the fiery love of God's Spirit laboring to set Christ's Mighties free.

Here's Paul's list: We are not to be "lovers of our own selves, covetous, boasters, proud, blasphemers, disobedient to parents, unthankful, unholy, without natural affection, trucebreakers, false accusers, incontinent, fierce, despisers of those that are good, traitors, heady, highminded, lovers of pleasures more than lovers of God; having a form of godliness, but denying the power thereof" (3:2-5).

We mustn't claim to stand for our King but then deny Him by living a fleshly existence. Our King's Mighties don't shy away from the blazing searchlight of God's Word, but rather, willingly expose their souls and cry, "Dear King, if there be anything that stands between You and me, if there be anything that shrouds Your glory, if there be anything that will weaken my sword in battle, purge it, slay it, utterly destroy it!"

This world needs to once again witness the Lord God of Jashobeam. They need to witness the invincible strength of a Christian born of the wisdom of God, a normal everyday person made superhuman by the impartation of God's mighty Spirit.

But Jashobeam is more than a picture of a king's warrior; he's a reminder to all of us miniature wannabe Mighties that this life and battle is deeply personal to our God. He is looking for heart-friends, men and women who will allow themselves to be patterned after the sacred mind of their King, throw worldly caution to the wind, and win for themselves an intimate and affectionate nickname from their beloved Commander and Chief.

I encourage you to come to your King, kneel in His presence, and submit your life unto His purposes. Attune the ears of your inner man to His kindly voice and don't be surprised if He were to share a special name with you, a name unknown to this bustling world about, a name that encapsulates the deep and warm love of your King and perfectly expresses it to your childlike heart.

Maybe you are His strong shield?

Maybe you are His dear watchman?

Maybe you are His beloved under-shepherd?

Could it be that you are His lamb? His rock? His fire? His prophet?

Maybe you are His friend? His beloved? The apple of His eye?

Or could it be that you are His David, His Joab, His Jashobeam, His 'Etsen 'Adiynow in this generation?

Why don't you, with trembling heart, enter into your awesome King's presence, kneel before Him, and find out?

# *a moment for prayer*
## HEAVEN'S WISDOM

### ❧ LESLIE ❧

I s it just me, or do these supernatural stories of spiritual heroism intrigue you as well? I just love the fact that Jashobeam is termed in Scripture as "the son of wisdom." How ironically hilarious it is that what this world looks at as utter stupidity (fighting single-handedly against 800) would go down in the biblical record under the banner of "wisdom."

But that is how the spiritual reality works. Everything about God's kingdom, God's way of doing things, flies in the face of this world's established methods.

Over the past couple years I've been forced to come to grips with the fact that I've mistaken, in many ways, earthly wisdom for God's wisdom. For instance, I'm one of those organic health-loving sorts of people. For the past 18 years I've been made fun of for my diet (which includes, but is not limited to, a variety of meat substitutes, rice milk, coconut oil, spelt bread, and carob chips). I'm used to all the teasing. But here's the funny thing: Even though people pick on my health choices, I end up being the "wise" one in the bunch because everyone else is rotting away their bodies on white bread and Hostess cupcakes.

To me, fretting over every last thing that enters my body has been a point of wisdom. I've even called it that—*wisdom*. After all, it doesn't seem very wise to cram things into my body that will break it down and leave it powerless to do its job here on Earth.

But let's match up my thinking over these past 18 years with God's wisdom.

In the book of Matthew, chapter 6, we see Jesus bring up the topic of eating for a quick discussion. But, surprisingly, right where I would have expected Him to plant a major warning about fried foods, high caloric intake, and a diet high in starches, He doesn't do it. Instead He turns the tables on me and my earthly wisdom and says (and I paraphrase for effect):

> Leslie, give not a single thought to how you will eat, what you will eat, and what the sugar content is in what you eat. Instead, turn your attentions to Me, live as I tell you to live, and make Me the entirety of your life. After all, you can trust that My Father in heaven knows full well that your body needs to function healthy and strong in order for you to do My work down here on Earth—so trust Me—your health is better off if I'm the one in charge of it, and not you!"[1]

It's funny how we can see clearly on some matters and be blind as a bat on others. Eric and I have been telling young people for years to not give a single anxious thought to their love lives, but rather, trust God to write their stories. And then there I was, fretting about my health, thinking that unless I monitored every little thing that goes in and out of my body, I was going to come down with some horrible disease. Well, that's the equivalent of feeling that if you don't marry the one jerk that has shown any interest and attraction for you that you will surely fritter the rest of your life away as a lone spinster.

Now there is certainly nothing wrong with eating responsibly, and I believe we *are* vulnerable to health issues if we become gluttons, eating mainly to indulge our flesh. But trying to ward off sickness by following every new health fad that comes onto the scene demonstrates an amazing lack of trust—and creates an incredible amount of bondage in a person's life. The world says, "You better take this pill or eat this amazing new health food if you want to stay strong!" But God says,

"Trust Me! I'm a lot bigger than you think I am. Please, just let Me be God in your life."

Every sphere of life has its wisdom, its laws, and its experts that sagaciously promote it. For instance, in the arena of eating there are loads of experts—from nutritionists, to herbalists, to chiropractors—who will fill your ear with all that you could possibly know to take control of this area of your life.

If the concern is eye trouble, then there is an opthomologist just down the road who can tell you precisely how to fix it.

Ear trouble? Try an otolaryngologist.

Feeling depressed? Try a psychologist, or maybe a physician who might find you the perfect drug to match your symptoms.

Need more confidence? Go to an image consultant.

Need more cash? Talk to an Amway salesman.

Need a marriage partner? Talk to eHarmony.

You get the idea. If there is a problem that you are experiencing here on Earth—a void, a disability, a fear, a shortage—there are experts just waiting to help dispense to you all the earthly wisdom your heart desires.

In every academic sphere, be it biology, botany, chemistry, psychology, physiology, physics, mathematics, aerodynamics, or atmospheric science—there is a set of inviolable rules, laws that each of these academic disciplines orbit around. And from the time of Adam and Eve, these rules have been in place. These rules are known as *natural law*.

To know biology, botany, or chemistry is not bad. Such knowledge can be wonderful. But to be *limited* to the knowledge of biology, botany, or chemistry causes one to be limited to the bounds of natural law in their thinking, reasoning, and ultimately, *their believing*.

You see, though God is the inventor of all the above-mentioned academic subjects, He also is a lot bigger than any and all of them. And He is not limited to the bounds of natural law in how He interacts with humans, nor with how He interacts with world events.

An opthomologist can address blindness only with natural wisdom and is bound by the restraint of natural law. But God is not limited to such a smallish worldview. He created the eyeball and He can, in direct response to prayer and faith, make that blind eye whole and perfect once again and able to see. That is something even the greatest earthly wisdom couldn't manufacture.

You see, Christians were never supposed to be mere students of biology, botany, or chemistry, and thus limited in their scope to the bounds of natural law. Christians are supposed to be students of heavenly law—and calibrate their expectations, their lifestyle, and their attitudes accordingly.

The Christian life is intended by God to be supernatural through and through. It is supposed to live on a different fuel than broccoli and cauliflower and the daily green shake. It is supposed to function on the fuel of faith.

The Christian is supposed to see the deaf, the mute, the depressed, the insecure, the indebted, and the unhappy single person and say to them, "Do you want some good news?"

We are not bound by the petty constraints of natural law. The rules of biology, botany, chemistry, psychology, physiology, physics, mathematics, aerodynamics, or atmospheric science can and will be trumped by our faith in God and through the power of wrestling prayer. Read the Old Testament if you don't believe it. Then read the life of Jesus. And then take a gander at the lives of the apostles. Then, if you are still having a difficult time swallowing such a notion, read Christian history.

Christians don't define their worldview and their thinking from men or women with PhDs. Rather, they define their worldview, thinking, and every expectation around the hugeness of their great God and around His perfect wisdom.

## Understanding the Wisdom of Heaven

Let's quickly evaluate how God's wisdom differs from the wisdom of this world:

*Problem:* You are in the midst of a battle and there are 800 hostile Philistines just up ahead wanting to eat you for lunch. And to make matters worse, *you are all by your lonesome.* What would human wisdom say? That's right—human wisdom would shout, "Run for your life, Jashobeam!"

*Solution:* But what does God's wisdom say? God's wisdom says, "Go fight them—I will be with you, and I will defeat them!"

*Problem:* Over 5000 men, women, and children are miles away from town, hungry, and desperately in need of food. What would human wisdom say? Yep. It would say, "Send them all home as quickly as possible and let them all find their own food."

*Solution:* But what does God's wisdom say? It says, "Does anyone have some food?" Then it does the most audacious thing—it prays over the handful of bread and fish that it collects and says, "Okay everyone, please be patient as we distribute a great feast to you."

*Problem:* We are out on a lake, and a terrible storm comes sweeping in from the north. The boat is rocking and water is filling up our fishing boat. What would human wisdom say? That's right—it would say, "Panic!" and then it would add, "Let's get out of here."

*Solution:* But what does God's wisdom say? It says, "Would anyone mind if I closed My eyes for a few minutes and catch a little shut-eye?" And then when everyone gets riled at such a notion, God's wisdom stands up in the boat and faces the storm head-on and commands, "Peace, be still!"

*Problem:* A multitude of sick, blind, maimed, deaf, and mute arrive at our church service and say, "Please help us!" What would human wisdom say? Yep. It would say, "I've got a great relationship with Dickenson Memorial Hospital just down the road—I send a lot of folks there. I'm sure I can talk with them about your situation and maybe they'll consider doing some pro bono work for you."

*Solution:* But what does God's wisdom say? It says, "Be made whole by the power vested in the mighty name of Jesus Christ!" Then when everyone is looking at you funny, it says to the crippled man who hasn't walked a lick in his entire life, "Stand up, mister, and start walking!" And if that doesn't offend the rest of the gawking crowd, then it walks up to the grave of a man who has been dead for four days and says, "Lazarus, come forth!"

Christianity is a higher science, a higher understanding of how the universe works. It's not bound by Earth's rules and laws; it reasons and calls its plays from God's outrageous playbook. If the Bible says it, then it's true to a Christian and he lives accordingly.

The people of this Earth are bound by its natural laws and can only rise as high as their knowledge and mastery of these natural laws can bring them. But Jesus came and entrusted us with the key to a life lived under a higher, heavenly law.

And if you haven't figured it out yet, this heavenly pattern of living is accessed via *prayer*. Prayer is the operative tool—it's the rope tied to all God's promises yanking this astounding reality to Earth.

If you want to succeed on Earth, then look no further than conventional earthly wisdom. But if you want to succeed in and amongst the heavenly order and amidst the Company of Heroes, then it's high time we all get ahold of some heavenly wisdom. Life is not about health, wealth, and earthly prosperity—it's about a King, His kingdom being established, and His glory being made evident in all the Earth.

God is saying, "Jashobeam, charge into the host of 800! I will be with you in battle!" And we look back at Him, as if we know so much more than He does, and say, "But God, that just isn't a *wise* maneuver."

Proverbs 21:22 says, "A wise man scaleth the city of the mighty, and casteth down the strength of the confidence thereof."

Let me repeat that again in case you might have skimmed the verse. A "wise" man scales the city of the mighty. What a statement! It's not the stupid man, but the wise man that goes headlong into the enemy's territory and scales the city walls. That's preposterously amazing!

It's time that we start letting God define the rules of this drama called life and let Him define what wisdom really is.

We want to grow the church through slick marketing campaigns, through "beer and brat" fests in the church parking lot, through hip worship music during the service, and the stylish implementation of Hollywood clips into our sermons. But God says, "If you want church to be as church should be, pray!"

We try to secure our financial future through college degrees, through sleepless nights in business school, through hobnobbing with those who can give us a step-up, and through selling our souls to the cares of this world. But God says, "Pray!"

We try to find lasting and meaningful romantic relationship by becoming obsessed with how we look, going to singles' night at our local church, and building a superglossy profile on an online Christian dating site. But God says, "Pray!"

We try to stay healthy and strong by eating organic, downing supplements, and imbibing thick pasty green drinks. But God says, "Pray!"

For all matters, all issues, all problems, all complications, God has the same answer.

*Pray!*

But that just doesn't make sense to us, does it? Admit it, it sounds "unwise." To *pray* instead of *solve* sounds like we are doing nothing, that we are shirking a duty, laying down on the job. But to pray is not the absence of work; it's a completely different sort of work. It's not an abandonment of the good, old-fashioned work ethic. Rather, it's a proper direction of it.

To pray is to acknowledge that our God is "able to do exceeding abundantly above all that we ask or think" (Ephesians 3:20).

To pray is to say to God, "You can do it! And, I know You want to do it!"

To pray is to say, "I know my God cares about even something as seemingly inconsequential as this. Because He wants every moment of my life tailored around His pattern and design."

To pray is to acknowledge that the heavenly reality is more real than the earthly one.

To pray is an act of biblical faith. It's a statement to the heavenlies that our personal, man-made methods for solving life are not sufficient, and that God has purchased us the ability to find our solution to every part of life in the grandness of His Son.

To pray is to honor God.

Prayer puts God in the position He deserves—that of King, Governor, Benign Controller, Possessor, Lord, and Master. Prayer gives God the avenue through which to change the world. He responds to prayer—that's His pattern, and thus prayer gives God His due, His position, and ultimately His glory!

To pray is the ultimate wisdom—the highest act, the most brilliant behavior, the most perfect expenditure of the human life.

## Expecting the Response of Heaven

But the question that lingers in the air on the issue of prayer is this: *Will it actually do anything?*

If you stand up against a troop of 800 Philistines, will prayer be sufficient for you?

When you pray over your handful of loaves and fish, is prayer enough to do the job?

When you are in your boat and the storm is raging, can prayer be depended upon as a real-life solution?

When the sick, the lame, the blind, the deaf, and the dying come to you and say, "Help me!" can you confidently say, "I've got just what you need!"?

This is what we all are concerned about. Can prayer really do for my life, and for the lives of others, what I've been taught can only be done through earthly natural means?

Well, just ask George Muller, Hudson Taylor, Rees Howells, Madame Guyon, William Booth, Amy Carmichael, R.A. Torrey, Jackie Pullenger, and John Wesley—men and women who lived supernatural lives because they believed prayer was a sufficient means of seeing their practical and physical needs met in this lifetime.

Now it would be a bit naïve to oversimplify life to nothing more than prayer. There are many dimensions to life, and prayer is only one very critical one. Practical real-world *action* is also a part of the Christian life. God doesn't just ask us to kneel in a prayer closet, we also are called to go out into this world and make disciples of all men. We are called to work hard, and practically live life. We are called to mind our health, pay our bills, and cultivate relationships (including marital ones). Prayer is not supposed to be *all* we do—it's just supposed to *undergird* all we do. Prayer is not supposed to be just the *first* thing we do, but the *first, second, fourth, seventh,* and *final thing* we do in each circumstance.

Prayer is supposed to be the governing and primary practical tool we use to live life, make decisions, and impact this Earth. We follow the lead of God and we know how to follow by spending time in prayer.

Jesus asks us to pray. He says, "Ask, seek, knock." This is His prescribed method for taking the riches of His kingdom, the power of His person, and the purchase of His cross and bringing it into living reality here on Earth.

But first, we must believe that God's pattern is the right pattern. And not just that it is the right pattern, but that it works.

God has already anticipated every feeble reason you are going to try to throw out in order to excuse yourself from this mighty calling. He says, "Leslie, take no thought." "Brian, that isn't your concern, it's My concern—you follow Me." "Kelly, My Father knows you will need that—don't fear; if you follow Me down the narrow way of obedience, I will ensure that you are taken care of."

Our God says, "Pray!"

Let's just agree with Him that His way, though it appears unwise to this world, is the highest wisdom known to man.

If He says, "Pray!" then I say we listen to our God and start praying.

# THE PASDAMMIM PARCEL
*yielding not an inch of the king's land*

Eleazar and Shammah—two of the three mightiest

⊰ ERIC ⊱

I've always been intrigued by the idea of heading off to military boot camp. Call me crazy, but there is something about the idea of having someone push me, try me, inspect me, call me out, and press me until I'm a battle-ready physical specimen that fascinates me. I love doing push-ups, I love running and running until I'm spent, and I love making my bed every morning—so in my mind it seems like a pretty good fit.

Leslie has never been very excited about me ditching her and the kids for three months just so that I can experience the thrill of boot camp, and as a result, I've never been able to find out what it is really like.

I don't like flab, whether it be on my body, in my mind, or in my soul. And though I don't like the flab, it sometimes can be difficult to rouse myself to get rid of it. Remember that statement about Christ's disciples in the garden of Gethsemane? "The spirit is indeed willing, but the flesh is weak" (Matthew 26:41). Boy, can I relate to that. There is a part of me that absolutely detests spiritual flab, but there is another part of me that grows foggy-minded and tired the moment I begin to address the issues in my inner life.

I may want to pray, but gadzooks am I tired right now!

I may want to study the Word, but first I think I might need to just close my eyes for 15 minutes.

I may want to reach out and help that needy person over there, but there is a strange reluctance within me that says, "Preserve your strength, Eric—if you spend it now on that guy you may not have enough for yourself later."

That's flab! It's a big, tirelike blubber-ring wrapping itself about the soul.

I might hate this blubber-ring, but its very presence prohibits me from even finding the spiritual energy to exercise it off.

I'm guessing that you too are familiar with this flab?

I personally detest flab. But hatred of flab itself doesn't remove flab. You can't "despise" spiritual flab any more than you can grumble and complain physical flab away. Flab leaves because it is systematically targeted, proactively attacked, and aggressively worked off the spiritual man.

God's Gibborim are lean, mean fighting machines. They are flab-less wonders, tireless superheroes. They are men and women who do not grow foggy and tired-minded the moment prayer is brought up in conversation. They are heroes who don't need a 15-minute nap when the battle for souls is at its most pivotal juncture. Rather, they are sharp of mind and sharp of heart—always alert, always watchful of their King's needs. The Mighties are men and women who stand awake when all others fall into a slumber.

The apostle Paul, the Jashobeam of his generation, demonstrated this extraordinary tireless existence. He made the outrageous claim that he was *tireless* in the cause of the gospel. When it came to spiritual tenacity, Paul "fainted not."[1] He claimed to pray without ever stopping.[2]

Just imagine such a life! Imagine never tiring in your passion, pursuit, or practical availability to your King. Imagine never exiting from a state of prayer, maintaining a constancy of connectedness to the issues pertaining to your beloved Commander.

This little diminutive man (the name *Paul* even means "little" or "small") lived an extraordinary existence. He didn't just make poetic statements about having a flabless life, he demonstrated it in living color. Just take a look at this snapshot of his superheroic existence:

> Five times I received from the Jews thirty-nine lashes. Three times I was beaten with rods, once I was stoned, three times I was shipwrecked, a night and a day I have spent in the deep. I have been on frequent journeys, in dangers from rivers, dangers from robbers, dangers from my countrymen, dangers from the Gentiles, dangers in the city, dangers in the wilderness, dangers on the sea, dangers among false brethren; I have been in labor and hardship, through many sleepless nights, in hunger and thirst, often without food, in cold and exposure. Apart from such external things, there is the daily pressure on me of concern for all the churches (2 Corinthians 11:24-28 NASB).

That's a list that makes even the toughest men grow tired. And yet, even with such weights, such obstacles, such persecutions, this mighty man refused to grow tired or weary. He refused to let go of his sword.

The Mighties are miracle men. They don't live according to the same fuel source as the rest of the men of their age. They have tapped into the tireless Spirit of the Almighty. The human body, mind, and heart can handle only so much before it cracks under the weight, breaks under the pressure, and collapses under the strain. But God is in the business of building men and women who don't crack, who don't break down, and who don't collapse when the battle is at its fiercest. He builds flabless warriors who run on an endless supply of supernatural soul fuel.

I realize this might sound preposterous, but if you have gotten this far into this book, I'm guessing that you could acknowledge that this whole Mighties concept is preposterous if looked at through the lens of the intellectual. Remember, these realities are unlocked and experienced only through boyish (or girlish) belief.

Jesus made it clear that His Mighties ought always to pray and never faint.[3]

Do you hear those words? Always pray. Never faint. Remember, this isn't Eric Ludy talking. This is your King.

Paul said, "We faint not [speaking of himself and the band of Mighties surrounding him]."[4] "And let us not be weary in well doing: for in due season we shall reap, if we faint not."[5]

He then went on to say, "Those things, which ye have both learned, and received, and heard, and seen in me, do."[6]

Paul was saying, "Everything I have, everything I do is available to you." That means the flabless life is accessible; it's there for the taking.

In the original Greek text, the word for what I'm terming "flab" is *ekkakeō*. It means "empty of the fighting spirit, exhausted, wearied, tired, faint."

And our King cannot have warriors that yield to *ekkakeō*. Your spiritual eyes may want to close and take a short little nap, but *never* give ground to *ekkakeō*. There is a supernatural fuel source that God has for His saints that you must learn to tap into.

Two years ago, almost to the day, Leslie prayed for me in this precise area. I have given myself radically and relentlessly into ministry for the last 17 years of my life. But I have grown tired; I have grown weary in well-doing. There have been times of such utter exhaustion. I can remember countless evenings where I have laid on the couch after a long day of pouring out and been unable to pray, been unable to keep my eyes open as my wife was attempting to talk with me. I was fighting, yes, but I was a flabby warrior. The battle was proving superior to my willing soul. And in the most important moments I was catatonic with fog and tiredness.

"Make my man tireless in battle, Lord!" Leslie prayed. "Give him that growl that never ceases, that heavenly soul fuel that keeps him awake to You always."

I had that yucky *ekkakeō* in my soul. And Leslie was crying out to

God on my behalf to see it removed, to see me roused to fight once again, but this time with a supernatural *grrrr* within my soul.

I'll never forget one of her specific prayers. It caught me off guard, but it massively altered my life.

"Enable Eric to pray like a man!" she pled. "Give him heat to his prayers, Lord!"

*Pray like a man?* What does that mean?

*Heat to my prayers?* What exactly does heat have to do with prayer?

Well, I soon found out.

Leslie's prayer started a new and deeper work within me. It was as if a fire burned within my soul and it had to express itself in flaming fiery prayer. When I would pray, from that day forward, I was moved by a stronger impulse, a greater anger toward sin, an expanded love for God's people—a more dynamic concern, a more passionate dog-gedness, *a greater heat.*

Since then, whenever Leslie and I enter into a time of intercessory prayer for others, I imagine grabbing ahold of the very same donkey jawbone that Samson utilized to slay the 1000 Philistines. I hold that sacred weapon in my spiritual grip and I growl within my soul, cov-enanting with my King that I will not run from the battle, but will keep swinging until every last Philistinian foe is vanquished. I look heavenward and call out for the fuel of heaven to fight the upcoming battle, and I predetermine that *ekkakeō* will not be allowed in, even to the slightest degree.

I fight until victory and refuse to grow weary.

Leslie and I always say to one another, "No downtime!" In other words, "No *ekkakeō*!" There is no allotment for even a moment of defeat, even a short period of haziness, even a brief escape into a spiri-tual vegetable state.

These past couple years I have had my moments when *ekkakeō* slipped briefly into my soul. There were times when my eyelids began to close, when that donkey's jawbone grew awfully heavy in my spiritual hand. But in every case, there was an inner growl that pronounced, *No downtime, Eric! No downtime!* I have spent two years refusing to excuse this *ekkakeō* in my inner life. I have two years drawing on a new energy source for the spiritual battle, and what a time it has been as a result!

My body and my mind were trained to habitually slip into a spiritual catatonic state periodically throughout the week. I was used to retreating to a movie, a book, a nap, a bowl of ice cream whenever *ekkakeō* came knocking. But God has been training my soul after a completely different pattern—a life that finds its full refreshment, full pleasure in the constant communion with my King. In those moments of suggested tiredness, instead of turning to a movie, a book, a nap, or that bowl of ice cream, He's inviting me to fuel up on Him and find an entirely new dimension of strength and stamina.

Leslie and I live *uncaffeinated* lives. In other words, we are not propped up throughout our day by a gallon of coffee, various stimulants, sugars, pain relievers, or sleeping aids. We live an existence energized by our natural human juices alone. However, over the past 14 years of marriage those "natural human juices" have proved inadequate for the immense spiritual battle we face day in and day out.

But I have discovered something extraordinary this past year.

There is God-fuel available. But this God-fuel only works in a soul that allows it to burn unmixed. There can be no props allowed. To enjoy this "spiritual tirelessness," a believer must come to God willing to let go of every other crutch, every other prop. He must allow God to be his strength, God to carry him through the battle, God to keep his eyelids open, and God to maintain the clarity of his mind.

About 23 months ago at the time of this writing, God began to prove the power of His fuel in me. I'll never forget the night. A precious member of our church community was being beaten down by the enemy. There was a grip of fear upon this person's life, and the battle was a fierce one. In fact, it was not just fierce *but long*. But whereas previously in my spiritual approach I had been willing to fight until my body began to cry out for mercy, in this situation I could sense that there was a victory waiting just up ahead, but I needed to press into God at a deeper level than I ever had before in order to get it.

I'm one of those guys who prefers to get to bed at 9:30. I love my sleep. In fact, in choosing to live "uncaffeinated" I rely on my sleep to get me through the next day. However, in this situation, God was saying, "I'm bigger than sleep. I can give you everything you need to be strong tonight *and* tomorrow. But you have to trust Me!"

Nine-thirty passed, and we kept wrestling in prayer. There was a keen sense amongst the group that victory was imminent.

Eleven o'clock passed. I was feeling a bit of tiredness, but I begged God to keep me focused and alert for this fight.

Midnight passed, and I found that even though victory was not yet achieved, there was an increasing strength, a growing confidence within me.

Two a.m. slipped on by and I was still standing, still pressing in, still praying prayers with heat.

At 2:30 something incredible happened. There was a breakthrough. It seemed the floodgates opened and an overwhelming joy gushed into this previously agonized soul. I was witnessing an amazing spiritual triumph of light over darkness—it was so beautiful, so majestic, and so extraordinary to watch.

I'd never seen anything quite like it before. I had always stopped praying when my body told me that it couldn't go on. And 9:30 is when my body starts squawking. Yet though we wrestled for eight hours straight, pressing in with fiery passion and swinging that jaw-bone about, there was something fueling the drama beyond "natural human juices."

Over the next few days, I encountered four more of these spiritual battles. It was as if God was drawing them out of the woodwork to train me. Each one seemed like the battle of the ages, and they were one on top of the other. There was no time for rest, no time for a little 15-minute catnap—there were human souls in the ascendant and God was saying, "Eric, you are My man!"

It was a three-day period that taxed my physical body, mind, and heart like very few things prior in my spiritual life—but whereas before I would have justified my needed departure from such hairy battles, this time I was all in, 100 percent, keenly focused, constantly swinging, heat never ebbing for even a short period from my prayers.

I was talking with one of my pastor friends in Denver the day following these five amazing victories.

I said, "Ben, I've never seen anything like this. I just decided that I would not let go until there was victory; I refused to yield to tiredness, and every single time God not only provided strength for the battle but there was radical triumph proven in the lives of everyone I prayed for!"

Ben was silent for an uncomfortable bit of time on the phone. Then he said, "Eric, God's been stirring this same thing in me. It's what the Christian men and women of yesteryear called *praying through*."

That was 23 months ago, and since that time Leslie and I have *prayed through* for countless people. We have spent an entire two years training in this precise area. Over and over again we enter into battle, I yank up that donkey jawbone and start swinging. Six, eight, ten, twelve hours straight sometimes. But in each situation, there is a refusal to give sway to *ekkakeō* in even the slightest degree, and there is a doggedness to pray until victory is achieved.

David and his Mighties carried swords and shields. They fought battles over physical territory. However, Jesus and His men are armed with an entirely different array of armament. Our weaponry is spiritual. But trust me, that doesn't mean that it is inferior.

As Scripture says in 2 Corinthians chapter 10, "The weapons of our warfare are...mighty" (verse 4).

We are not left helpless in battle, but are given weaponry that is stronger and more powerful than the tools that David and his Mighties utilized. David and his men fought physical enemies, but we are privileged to fight the root spiritual powers that puppeteer our physical enemies in order that even our enemies might be set free to become friends of God.

God can provide us with the weaponry to destroy the controlling faction of lust in a man's life. We can rush on the gates of pride and carry them off just as Samson carried off the gates of Gaza. We can scale and overcome the walls of laziness. We can crush the strong man of fear with the authoritative sledgehammer of prayer.

*Tenacity.*

Isn't that a great word? It denotes clinging, never yielding, holding on, persisting through the toughest times. Tenacity is one of the main ingredients in the recipe for the Mighties. Leaving it out would be akin to forgoing the flour in the recipe for making bread. Bread is just not bread without flour. And neither is a Mighty a true Mighty without a tenacious spirit.

There is a brief story in the Bible in both 1 Chronicles 11 and 2 Samuel 23. It's a seemingly innocuous story—that is, until you realize why it was put there. It was placed within the Bible because it demonstrates an oft-overlooked dimension of the heart of God.

It's a dimension that, for the sake of our discussion herein, let's call *tenacity.*

As the story goes, there is a field of barley and beans, a parcel of land known in the Bible merely as *Pasdammim*, or "the boundary of blood." This little parcel of land was abandoned by the Israelites, who fled before an incoming flood of Philistines. The field didn't seem important enough to protect, but it was there that David stood. And it says in the Bible that though all the other Israelites had fled, Eleazar and Shammah stood with David and fought.

They fought for what the other Israelites deemed a worthless parcel of barley and beans. But to the king, this parcel was everything. It was territory entrusted to him by God, and he dared not yield even an inch of it.

Eleazar defied the Philistines. It says that "he arose, and smote the Philistines until his hand was weary, and his hand clave unto the sword: and the LORD wrought a great victory that day; and the people returned after him only to spoil" (2 Samuel 23:10).

I absolutely love this picture. For it says that he fought until his hand was weary. He fought until an overwhelming degree of *ekkakeō* was knocking upon the door of his soul, but in that moment it says that "his hand clave unto the sword." What a statement! In that moment when his body was begging him to drop his sword, it says that "his hand clave," which could maybe be better understood as "his hand burned with unyielding resolve unto the hilt of his sword."

There are countless parcels of barley and beans in our lives. There is territory in our souls that rightfully belongs to our King and yet the enemy is occupying it or is desiring to occupy it.

It is here that our King stands His ground, unwilling to give even an inch of your life away, or an inch of any of His children's lives away. And it is here that He asks us to stand with Him—to stand in a place where all other Christians seemed to have abandoned and claimed it either "Impossible!" or "Definitely not worth it!"

It's simply easier to live with flab wrapped about our souls. It's easier to flee in the time of testing than to stand our ground and cleave unto the hilt of our sword. It's easier to surrender in the day of temptation and crumble beneath the weights of lust and laziness. It's easier to look at the pornography than it is to turn away. It's easier to grow tired after a long hard day than it is to rouse ourselves on the fuel of the Spirit of God to keep fighting.

Let's admit it. Flab feels good.

But no matter how good this flab feels, it stands between you and your destiny as a Mighty Warrior in Christ's kingdom.

Flab is an enemy to God's purposes in your life.

Jesus Christ is jealous for every square inch of your inner life, and therefore He is against any and all flab. He doesn't want even the slightest portion of your soul lost to the Philistines. It might seem like an unimportant parcel of barley and beans, but to your God that little parcel represents the most important piece of the kingdom of heaven today.

Your King is saying, "Do you see this spot of darkness right here in your soul? Stand with Me today and let's take it back for My glory!"

Your King is saying, "Do you see how your thoughts wander and give sway to lustful imaginings? Stand with Me today and let's claim your every thought for My purposes!"

Your King is saying, "Do you see how you grow tired right when the spiritual battle is raging the hottest? Stand with Me today and let Me give you heavenly fuel to eliminate all this yucky *ekkakeō*. Let's fight together until the victory is realized, and let Me train your soul to fight with tireless unction."

*Tenacity.*

Do you have it? If not, do you want it? If you do have it to a degree, do you want more?

God's Gibborim are miracle men; they are tireless wonders. They don't live lives built after the blueprint of Suburbia, USA—but rather, after the heroic pattern of ancient times.

As a reminder, we read in Hebrews chapter 11 that these ancient men subdued kingdoms, wrought righteousness, obtained promises, stopped the mouths of lions, quenched the violence of fire, escaped the edge of the sword, out of weakness were made strong, waxed valiant in fight, turned to flight the armies of the aliens.

Is this the testimony of your life? Is this what might be shared about you in your eulogy were you to die today?

Remember, the name of that seemingly insignificant parcel of ground is interpreted to mean "the boundary of blood." Blood was shed in Israel in order that a little parcel of barley and beans might be preserved for the king.

In many ways, you and I are that little parcel of barley and beans. We may appear insignificant to this world about us, but we are not insignificant to our King. Maybe everyone has fled, pronouncing our life to not be worth the expenditure of their blood. Maybe there is no one willing to fight for us. However, it is right smack in the center of our seemingly insignificant souls that our King stands and proclaims, "I shed blood for this piece of territory—here I stand!"

Our King has fought for us. He has shed His own blood, thus making our inner parcel of barley and beans of inestimable value in the heavenlies.

Eleazar and Shammah weren't distracted by the barley and the beans. They didn't spend time pondering the worthiness of such a fight. Rather, they fought because the king they loved said, "Here I stand, men! This is important to me!"

Whatever is important to our King instantly becomes important to His Mighties. And the reverse is true as well, for anything that our King deems a waste is instantly deemed a waste by His Mighties.

The single-eyed pursuit of wealth and earthly treasure is scoffed by our King—and therefore we should scoff it too. It's a waste of a life.

The single-eyed pursuit of earthly importance, fame, and power is ridiculed by our King—and therefore we too should hold it with low regard. For it too is a waste of a life.

However, justice and mercy are prized in our King's mind.

The poor, the orphan, the widow, the outcast, the imprisoned, the lonely, the oppressed, the enslaved, the disabled, and the foreigner are cherished as the royalty in His kingdom caste system.

He weeps over the souls of the lost. Shouldn't we?

He says that purity, holiness, love, compassion, and truth are precious in His economy and entirely worthy of a life's pursuit.

He claims that children, innocence, sacred femininity, holy Scripture, and sound doctrine are without hesitation worthy of dying to protect.

No matter whether any of these things seem important to our natural minds, these are things that our King deems important!

It's as if Jesus is saying, "These may appear to be but a parcel of barley and beans to this world, but these each fall inside My boundary of blood! And if these were worth My blood, they are without a doubt worth the blood of My Mighties!"

It says of Eleazar that "his hand clave unto the sword."

What is your hand holding on to?

Are you holding on to your reputation, your comforts, or your way of doing things?

A true Mighty is willing to let go of everything to grab ahold of Jesus and to cleave to Him.

Are you holding on to your wisdom, your abilities, your aptitude, or even your position in this world?

There is a sharp, strong weapon of God, known as Jesus Christ, being held out to you right now. The hilt of this sword is hot with holiness. To grab ahold of it will certainly cause great pain and an entire renovation of your existence. But please don't pass up such an opportunity to join this sacred order of Heroes. Please don't pass over this privilege to be inducted into the league of Mighties.

Grab ahold of your King!

*Tenacity.*

It will change your soul; it will change this world.

# *a moment for prayer*
## TENACITY

### ⅋ LESLIE ⅋

There are some things Eric and I have prayed about for over 15 years, and we still haven't seen the answers come. Then there are other things that we prayed about for two minutes and saw the answers immediately.

American culture trains us to be in a hurry. Everything is instant, and that "instant" expectation has a tendency to warp our view of prayer. You see, prayer is participation in a very real battle. And depending on the thickness of the enemy resistance at the precise point you are addressing in prayer, the answer may not come quickly. In fact, there are some prayers with answers that have taken thousands of years to come to fruition (the coming of the Messiah, for one).

One of the most common complaints about prayer is that it doesn't work: "I tried praying."

This is a pitifully weak and all-too-common excuse to give up on wrestling prayer.

I'm going to go out on a limb and make what may seem a preposterous statement:

Prayer *always* works!

I realize that sounds a little too Pollyannaish in its optimism and its seeming disregard for reality. But let me explain.

For most of us, our beef with the powerlessness of prayer is actually a beef with the powerlessness of unbiblical prayer. Because, prayer, as built after the biblical pattern, *works*—it's that simple.

There are three things that I would propose make up the recipe for true prayer. All three ingredients are not always required for prayer to be answered, but any prayer sincerely offered up in keeping with all three of the following ingredients has never, in all of world history, not been answered. Let's explore the key ingredients:

*Ingredient #1*—**Praying God-prayers.** I mentioned this in chapter 6. God wants to tutor us in not just *how* to pray, but *what* to pray. When a believer prays "God-prayers," then it provides tremendous grounds for ingredient #2 to get mixed in...

*Ingredient #2*—**Praying with complete confidence (aka—faith).** Doubt is a prayer killer. It's like tying a 100-pound dumbbell to the ankle of your prayer and trying to get it to float heavenward. The Christian should be just as assured in God's desire to answer his prayer as he might be assured that the sun will rise tomorrow and the sky will still be blue. God's nature is a guarantee, and as part of that revealed nature, He has told us that if we ask, in accordance with the "recipe" (as summarized here), our prayers will be heard. As children of God, we have every reason to be confident in our praying.

*Ingredient #3*—**Praying until the answer comes.** This one's the kicker. And this is the point where most people who start out with God-prayers and God-confidence end up with the illusion of unanswered prayer. Leaving out ingredient #3 is the equivalent of de-toothing a tiger and wondering why the thick, juicy steak sitting in front of him has gone uneaten. Persistence is the heart of prayer; it's the doggedness of importunance that gets the job done in the heavenlies.

Ingredient #1 gives the reason for the praying (let's add one cup). Ingredient #2 is the key that opens heaven's vault (add two cups). But ingredient #3 is the guts of faith—it's the heart of Christianity, it's the real-life stuff of heroes, and it's what proves the soul of the wrestler (add three cups).

Now, to be fair, God has been known to answer prayers that were nothing more than raw cries of faith from an anguished soul. There was nothing purposeful or thought through about the prayers; they were sincere and hot with the emotion of desperation.

This is not to say God can't answer prayers that rise up out of the wash of ignorance or the ash of selfishness—it's to say that God is not bound to answer such prayers.

But God is *bound* to answer the prayers of those saints who seek Him as He has asked to be sought. Our God is a prayer-answering God. He's not a God who picks and chooses to answer the prayers that sound the wisest, or the most verbose, or, for that matter, the most spiritual. He answers every single prayer when it is prayed as He has prescribed. And that's not to insinuate that He is picky. Just as steel beams sink when placed in water, God knows that wood floats, and so He says, "Use wood when building your boat, Noah." That does not mean God is picky; it simply means He knows what works.

And so God says, "Pray to Me this way—because I really want you to be successful!"

Our God is not looking for a reason to *not* answer our prayers. He is eager to help us, but He asks us to do it *His* way and not ours. And God's way demands that you hang in there, not for just a few rounds, but all 16—until the knockout finally comes, or the victory is achieved.

God highly esteems the persistent soul. When talking about prayer, Jesus used the illustration of the persistent widow asking, and asking, and asking until the wicked judge gave in to her request (Luke 18:2-8). Then Jesus talked about the importunate neighbor who kept knocking, and knocking, and knocking until his neighbor opened up and gave him his request (Luke 11:5-10). And Jesus' interaction with the Syrophoenician woman in Matthew chapter 7, demonstrated yet again the simple principle that faith mixed with persistence equals results with our God.

But this is definitely not just a New Testament thing. Faithful persistence is the essence of the entire Bible. In fact, as we mentioned earlier, the name *Israel* (the official name for God's people) demonstrates this very fact with beautiful clarity.

As the story in Genesis chapters 25 through 32 goes, Jacob had been seeking the blessing of God since birth (literally). And by hook or crook, he was going to get it. But finally, after all his attempts to gain it by his own cunning and strength, he comes to the end of himself. And in a state of great desperation, he arrives one night at a place called *Peniel* (which means "the face of God"), and it is there that he meets God face-to-face.

Jacob, in his desperation, grabs ahold of God. And we read that he wrestled with God. He knew that what he needed was not going to be found anywhere but with the One he was clinging to. And so he wouldn't let go. Scripture says that Jacob wrestled "until the breaking of the day" (32:24). He wrestled until the light came.

God said to him, "Let go!"

But Jacob said, "I will not let go until You bless me."

He knew God had what he needed, and he was not willing to end this wrestling match without that enduement, that power from his God.

Most of us have never even come to Peniel. We do our praying and our Christian thing in our own cunning and strength. But Peniel is the place where spiritual things truly get done. It's the place of wrestling, and that intimidates many of us. It's the place of holding on until the day breaks, until the victory is achieved—and that sounds tiresome. But this is the great secret to answered prayer.

God was so moved by this wrestling interchange with Jacob that He gave the tired, limping wrestler a new name. He said, "I will now call you Israel! Because you have grabbed ahold of your God and didn't let go until you prevailed."

The very name of God's people denotes this idea of wrestling. It's the infrastructure of this whole gospel business. God's people are overcomers; they are champions; they are travailing prevailers. They are those who find the treasure and then go and sell all to secure it. They are those who see the glory of their God and then wrestle in prayer until that glory is seen in all its fullness here on Earth.

This is the stuff of revival. It's continuing to ask until the awakening, the stirring, the power comes.

Seven long years of persistence and wrestling prayer went by before William Carey baptized his first convert in India. Seven years of hardship and wrestling prayer went by before Adoniram Judson won his first disciple in Burma. It was the same arduous passage of time for Robert Morrison before he introduced a Chinaman to Christ. And Robert Moffat tells the exact same tale—seven long, hard years before the first evident moving of the Holy Spirit upon his Bechuanas of Africa. And yet again, it was seven hard years of importunate wrestling prayer before Henry Richards wrought the first convert gained at Banza Manteka.

Seven years? Is there a modern-day man or woman of God who is willing to wrestle seven long years, with no apparent fruit, until the breaking of day? Each of these stories—Carey, Judson, Morrison, Moffat, and Richards—mentions hard years of wrestling before the benefits of such persistence were discovered. Only then did each of these missionaries find earthshaking revival.

Leonard Ravenhill said, "Unction is God's knighthood for the soldier-preacher who has wrestled in prayer and gained the victory."[1]

Count Zinzendorf despaired over the tepid and spiritual anemic condition of the Moravians, but he roused himself to wrestle in the power of the Spirit of God until change took place. When "suddenly, revival came at about eleven o'clock on the Wednesday morning of August 13th, 1727. Then began the Moravian revival, in which a prayer meeting was born that we are told lasted one hundred years. From that meeting came a missionary movement that reached the ends of the earth."[2]

I said at the beginning of this section that Eric and I have been wrestling for over 15 years to see certain things happen without, as of yet, a clear answer to our many hours of prayer. But that doesn't mean we are going to get discouraged and throw up our hands. We will press in all the more, knowing that today may very well be the day the sun breaks forth and the victory is gained.

Eric and I don't believe there is such a thing as unanswered prayer. There are misguided prayers, selfish prayers, and doubting prayers, but true prayer doesn't go unanswered—it is merely abandoned prematurely due to a lack of persistence and faithful endurance.

*But doesn't God sometimes say no?* Many Christians struggle with this question. And often, it's a huge stumbling block to wrestling prayer. When God doesn't appear to respond to our request after one or two prayer sessions, we assume He's said no and we move on. But Eric and I have come to understand that as we learn to pray in accordance with the Spirit of God—to pray the prayers that He lays on our hearts to pray—we can be confident the answer will not be no. When a prayer is truly inspired by Him, we have learned not to give up after the first or second plea, but to wrestle until His purposes are accomplished. There is an incredible picture of this in Christ's ministry—the case of the woman who came to Jesus on behalf of her daughter. E.M. Bounds retells the story beautifully:

> The case of the Syrophoenician woman…is a notable instance of successful importunity (persistence)…At first, Jesus appears to pay no attention to her agony, and ignores her cry for relief. He gives neither eye, nor ear, nor word. Silence, deep and chilling, greets her impassioned cry. But she is not turned aside, nor disheartened. She holds on. The disciples, offended at her unseemly clamor, intercede for her, but are silenced by the Lord's declaring that the woman is entirely outside the scope of His mission and His ministry. But neither the failure of the disciples to gain her a hearing nor the knowledge—despairing in its very nature—that she is barred from the benefits of His mission, daunt her, and serve only to lend intensity and increased boldness to her approach to Christ. She came closer… falling at His feet, worshiping Him and making her daughter's case her own cries, with pointed brevity, "Lord, help me!" This last cry won her case; her daughter was healed in the selfsame hour. Hopeful, urgent and unwearied, she stays near the master, insisting and praying until the answer is given. What a study in importunity, in earnestness, in persistence, promoted and propelled under conditions which would have

disheartened any but a heroic, constant soul. (Jesus) teaches that an answer to prayer is conditional upon the amount of faith that goes to the petition. To test this, He delays the answer. *The superficial prayer-er subsides into silence, when the answer is delayed. But the man of prayer hangs on, and on.* The Lord recognizes and honors his faith, and gives him a rich and abundant answer to His faith evidencing, importunate prayer (emphasis added).[3]

It is common to pray, "Lord if it is Your will, do this or that." But often this keeps us from being bold and specific in our praying. If we are always unsure whether we are praying in accordance with His will, then we will not have the confidence to wrestle until the break of day. It is true that we must pray in alignment with God's will in order to receive answers. But we often overlook the fact that anything that is in alignment with His nature is in accordance with His will. We don't need to wonder whether or not God wants to give us freedom from sin, power over the enemy, perfect peace, exceeding joy, strength for ministry, strong relationships, health in our marriages, and fruitfulness in His kingdom. These are things He makes very clear in Scripture that He delights to give us. (And the more we learn to listen to the still, small voice of His Spirit, the more we learn what His will is even in regard to the specific details of our lives. No longer do we merely pray our own prayers, but we pray the things that are on His heart to pray, in agreement with His Spirit—see Romans 8:26.)

To be honest, it makes me a little uncomfortable to make such bold statements about the manifold blessings of God, because I have seen many professing Christians abuse this principle, asking God to give them the selfish cravings of their flesh. (Like the "name-it, claim-it" people who think that if they ask in faith for a Lamborghini, God will give it to them.) Scripture makes it clear that if we are living for selfish pleasure instead of for Christ, we will not receive the things we ask for: "You ask and do not receive, because you ask amiss, that you may spend it on your pleasures" (James 4:3 NKJV).

But if we have yielded our entire heart, mind, and body to the Spirit of Christ, and are allowing Him to have rulership over our life, we can be confident that He desires to give us "everything we need for life and godliness" (see 2 Peter 1:3). He gives us good gifts not so that we can keep the benefits of His kingdom to ourselves, but so that we are strong to pour out those blessings on behalf of people in need. He blesses us so that we can be a blessing to others:

> I will bless you and make your name great; and you shall be a blessing (Genesis 12:2 NKJV).

> God is able to make all grace abound toward you, that you, always having all sufficiency in all things, may have an abundance for every good work (2 Corinthians 9:8 NKJV).

If you ever hesitate to bring your requests to God, remember that He is a loving Father. Just watching Eric's pleasure in meeting our children's daily needs for love, affection, food, clothes, sleep, etc. makes me realize how much God enjoys blessing us with His good gifts. He goes above and beyond our expectations. As Martin Luther said, "Whenever I have prayed earnestly, I have always received more than I have asked for."

When we ask our Father for bread, He will not give us a stone.

So don't grow weary in well doing. In due season you will reap a tremendous crop, if you *faint not*.

# THE SNOWY PIT
## *giving up the high ground to ensure an even greater victory*

Benaiah—captain of the king's bodyguard

⇥ ERIC ⇤

There is such a thing as self-built heroes, and there is such a thing as God-built heroes.

*Self-built* heroes are the glory of humanity. They earn themselves the applause of this Earth, for they have demonstrated that an earthly man or woman can prove valor, worth, and virtue without the aid of God through sheer discipline, human genius, and work ethic. This world esteems self-built heroes above all others.

*God-built* heroes are the glory of God. They earn themselves the applause of heaven, for they prove that the God of the universe is still willing and able to overtake the existence of a childlike believer and demonstrate the very nature, power, might, and love of God in and through human skin. This world despises God-built men and women above all others, for they prove in their very manner, life, and calling the existence of the Almighty.

There is no such thing as a self-built man or woman amongst God's elite band of Mighties. There is only one sort of hero allowed onto the hallowed honor roll of His heroes: *God-built* ones.

Benaiah, whom I must admit is possibly my favorite of David's Mighties, is such a God-built man. In fact, even his name, in the

Hebrew language, means "built by God." He was a spectacle of God's nature, power, might, and love on planet Earth.

Scripture says of Benaiah that he slew lions and giants.

God-built heroes are built to look identical to the One building them.

The list of mighty exploits performed by Benaiah reads longer than that of any other mighty man in the confidences of King David. This man's accomplishments were astounding. And not only was he named amongst the six most mighty of David, but he was *the* most mighty man in Solomon's (David's son) armed forces.

We read in 2 Samuel 8:18 that "Benaiah the son of Jehoiada was over both the Cherethites and the Pelethites."

The Cherethites and Pelethites were no insignificant thing in the kingdom of David. These guys were the ancient equivalent of the Secret Service. And Benaiah was their captain. First Chronicles 11:25 says, "David set him over his guard." He was personally responsible for protecting his king's body from harm. He was the chief sentinel, the captain of the royal bodyguard. His entire life's work was to preserve the integrity of his king's health.

He had to watch everyone, everything. He had to scrutinize every act, every word, every gift, and examine every motive. His king had a million enemies in this hostile world, and it was his job to sniff them out and to recognize them long before they ever reached the inner sanctum of David's confidences.

Benaiah had to prove loyal with every thought, every action. For possibly no one else in all the kingdom of David had a job more dependent on absolute and unwavering loyalty and purity of allegiance.

For years I've prayed for God to prove me for such a position of fealty in His kingdom. I've asked myself:

"Eric, is every thought loyal to the crown of Christ?"

"Eric, do you have the purity of soul necessary for such an illustrious position?"

I have seen in myself, over the years, traitorous thoughts that favor

self over Christ. I have sniffed attitudes of betrayal within my soul that
wish to yield to unbelief, doubt, discouragement, and fear, as well as
harbor sentiments that seek my own glory and applause. I have watched
myself subtly place distance between myself and Christ when popularity with this world was at stake.

I detest such weakness within me and I have yearned with every
fiber of my being to see these rebellious thoughts wholly and completely
removed. For as long as any of them remain, the position of Benaiah
cannot be mine. I wish to be a God-built man through and through.
I long for my every thought to be marked by purity, my every action
to be governed by the love of God, and my every decision to be ruled
by unabashed faith in my King.

To become a sentinel for the body of Christ demands a mind, a
heart, and a body wholly set apart and consecrated for such sacred
work. It demands rigorous loyalty of soul—a meticulous purity of
heart and mind.

Just as David had a million enemies in his day, Jesus has a billion
enemies today. There are countless assassination attempts plotted against
His truth and His body daily. There are many wolves masquerading
as sheep attempting to worm their way into the sheep pen. There are
numerous foes who monitor the walls of the city of God daily looking for breaches through which they can covertly slip in under the
banner of truth and delude the masses.

Benaiah was a man built by God for such a sacred position within
the king's government.

Is it possible that such a man or woman could be raised up today?
Is it conceivable that such a man of rigorous loyalty and meticulous
purity might once again stride onto the stage of life, or a woman in
whom the heart of the King can fully trust?

The answer is a resounding *yes!*

Even in his generation, Benaiah was certainly not the only man
responsible for the protection of his king's body. In fact, Benaiah led
an entire league of warrior-men, the Cherethites and the Pelethites,
who made up the royal bodyguard. And each of these lionlike men

had to first pass the "Benaiah test" before he was able to labor in such a sacred position of trust.

Could you pass the Benaiah test?

Just imagine the captain of the king's bodyguard setting you down for an interview. He looks you up and down with a careful gaze. He's thinking to himself, *Does he have the stuff?* Then he begins to ask you questions. Questions that even you don't think to ask yourself.

"Where do your loyalties lie?"

"Do you serve this king for money or for love?"

"Do you have a price tag? Is there a price at which your allegiance might be purchased?"

"Do you allow ungoverned thoughts to roam free inside your mind? Do you entertain anything in your thought life that violates the nature of your king?"

"Are you cowardly in your loyalties to your king when popularity with this world is in question? Or are you willing to be the only one standing with him if everyone else on planet Earth turns against him?"

"Are you ready to take a bullet for the body of your king?"

"Do you realize that if ever the body of your king is endangered that it is your duty to spill your blood to preserve it?"

"Do you realize that the standards of purity and holiness that the royal bodyguard are held to are higher and more stringent than those for the common man? Do you realize that these sacred standards will never be diminished and that there will be no reprieve from the searchlight of the Spirit of God upon your soul as long as you remain bonded to your king?"

The "Benaiah test" may seem extreme. But it is nothing more than the induction into the hallowed halls of Christ-built living.

Each of us as believers is called to join the ranks of the Cherethites and the Pelethites.

The King's body is under attack in our modern age. There are a billion foes seeking to undermine the integrity of the gospel, the purity of Christ's truth, and the holiness of His church.

The Mighties are for such a time as this. The Mighties are men and women born for valiance, crafted for battle, and groomed for utter and spotless loyalty. The Mighties are like Benaiah—*they are built by God!*

God builds His loyalists after the pattern of Benaiah. He trains them to have an inscrutable eye—to watch everyone, everything. To monitor every thought that knocks upon the human mind, to scrutinize every emotion that clangs on the door of the human heart. Every act, every word, every gift, and every motive is observed. For our souls, just like our Christ, have a billion enemies in this hostile world, and it is our job as the bodyguard of Christ to sniff out these enemies and to recognize them long before they ever reach the inner sanctum of our souls, our family's souls, our friend's souls, and the sacred confidences of the church.

Benaiah had to prove loyal with every thought, every action—*and so do you.* For the job Christ has called you to fulfill is identical to the job Benaiah had under David. And this job demands an absolute and unwavering loyalty unto your Christ and a purity of allegiance unto His kingdom and glory.

Benaiah might seem a bit larger than life. But which man mentioned in this book hasn't seemed a bit overblown and exaggerated? The very essence of God's Gibborim is "bigger-than-life" living. For the Mighties are all about Jesus. They are supernatural heroes, miracle men, heavenly women. They demonstrate Jesus. They speak of Jesus. They unlock the mysteries of Jesus. They prove the might and power of Jesus.

It says in the Bible that while snow lay on the ground in Israel, Benaiah trudged out into the chilly, hostile weather and found a lion trapped in a pit.

Human wisdom would say, "Stay indoors, Benaiah! Remain by the warmth of the fire!"

But, like David, like Joab, like Jashobeam, like Eleazar, and like Shammah before him, Benaiah was governed by a completely different sort of wisdom—a seemingly reckless confidence, a swagger that seemed to throw caution to the wind.

Human wisdom would say, "If you, by chance, stumble across a desperate, hungry lion trapped in a pit, let him be!" If you choose not to stay warm and indoors on a frigid icy day, then at least leave the lion, trapped in a pit, alone.

So what did our hero do?

Well, as strange as this might sound, *he jumped into the pit.*

That's right. Our hero had the high ground, he had the position on the wild beast, but he gave it up to prove his strength. He entered down into the pit (in a time of snow, mind you) and destroyed the lion.

Who does this sound like to you?

This is a picture of our King Jesus!

For all practical purposes, our King should have just stayed at home in heaven. After all, this world was in a time of sinful storm and the Earth was blanketed with an icy freeze. But not only did our King give up His heavenly home, He gave up His "high ground" and entered down into the pit. He was born as a baby to prove that even in His most fragile weakness He could decimate the roaring lion known as death, hell, and Satan.

We read of Benaiah that he slew an enormous, eight-foot-tall Egyptian warrior. This Egyptian giant rushed on Benaiah with a massive wooden spear, intending to destroy him. But Benaiah, with only a staff in his hands, stripped the great weapon from the giant's grip and plunged the massive spear into the Egyptian—killing him and causing all who beheld the mighty feat to stand in awe and wonder.

This Benaiah guy was something else. His entire life is a reminder of the might and the brawn of our Christ.

Jesus went up to Jerusalem, which is spiritually called Sodom and Egypt, and there the great giant sin and death awaited with a massive wooden cross in his hands. But Jesus—silent, naked, and with the meekness of a lamb—wrenched the blood-drenched weapon from the slimy hands of the devil and plunged it into Satan's gut—destroying the power of sin, the power of death, and defeating all the powers of the dark world forever.

I for one, stand in awe and wonder as I ponder such a mighty feat.

Benaiah, while he lived and breathed on this Earth, was in the business of his king. And as long as he remained in the business of his king, and made the king's life and body his priority, he shared in the strength, the might, and the heroics of his beloved commander.

The Spirit that built Benaiah so many thousands of years ago is searching to and fro throughout our generation looking for men and women to fill the ranks of the modern-day Cherethites and Pelethites. God is willing to build you and me into such lionlike sentinels, but first we must make the King's business our business. First, we must allow the bright searchlight of the Spirit of God to examine us, test us, and purify us for the sacred office of a true believer.

Imagine if the believers of our day were willing to be stretched into such a mold.

Imagine if the believers of our day were willing to hold up their souls before the Almighty and say with King David, "Search me, O God, and know my heart: try me, and know my thoughts" (Psalm 139:23).

Imagine if the pure and loyal spirit of Benaiah was allowed to course through the veins of the church once again.

Imagine if today's believers allowed themselves to be fashioned into sentinels for their souls, marriages, children, and churches, as well as the purity of doctrine and the integrity of Scripture.

Imagine such mighty Christianity once again on planet Earth!

# *a moment for prayer*
## RADICAL WILLINGNESS

What is it that hinders your prayer life? We all typically have a few major disturbances and then a whole host of small ones.

Sleep issues tend to be a leading contributor to dwindling prayer time. Poor management of time also ranks quite high on the list of prayer-robbers. Oh, and if I don't mention busyness, then this wouldn't be a very good short list. Of course, lack of a real desire to pray, general confusion as to how one is supposed to pray, and fear that prayer won't work (and thus faith in God will be shipwrecked) are all very real saboteurs as well.

Let's look at each of these major detractors and see what can be done about them.

## Detractors from Prayer

### Sleep

If you are anything like Eric and Leslie Ludy, then you probably cling to your sleep the way a hungry dog clings to his steak bone. The two of us really struggled with this whole sleep issue as God began to press us forward in prayer.

I remember how challenged Eric and I were when we read about William and Catherine Booth (founders of the Salvation Army) staying up through the night praying, pleading, and begging God for the power needed to truly minister the gospel on the following day.

To stay up through the night praying had never even entered our minds before. After all, we read in the Psalms that God gives His beloved rest. We were sure God wanted us to get our needed allotment of sleep each night…didn't He?

It was funny how this issue really bothered both of us. The very thought was almost offensive. It was as if we drew a line in the sand of our lives and said, "God, You can have all these hours in our day, then once we lay our heads on our pillows, we're sorry, but You will have to wait to take back control until we wake up again in the morning."

I personally believe that sleep is a very good thing emotionally, psychologically, physically, and spiritually. However, the unwillingness to give our sleep time over to God poses a huge obstacle to prayer. Some of the most sincere prayer is done when night falls and when bedtimes pass by because such a version of prayer purifies the motives and diminishes the flesh. It forces one to rely on God for supernatural fuel to pray with strength when the body is used to being weak.

This sleep issue also pokes at a very real piece of our lives that is not yet governed by the Spirit of God. You can always tell when God is in control of an area of your life because there is no fight to obey when the asking comes.

"Leslie, will you stay up tonight and share the hours with Me in prayer?"

When I wriggle at such a question, inwardly squirm, and seek a makeshift rationalization why it would be better for God if I didn't obey, it demonstrates that self is still very much alive in that area of my life. However, if I find myself seeing such an invitation from God as a great opportunity to spend intimate hours of closeness with my King, it is, instead, a demonstration that the Spirit is very much alive in the arena of my sleep.

It has been only two years since Eric and I began to make our nights available to God, so we are by no means experts at this. But, the simple decision to offer up our nights for the discretionary use of our God has caused our prayer lives to explode with a new energy and success. Suddenly, another eight hours opened up in our schedule for the possibility of prayer if God would so desire to use it.

So, you may be wondering how often God takes us up on this "nighttime prayer" thing. Well, I would say that over the past two years we have probably "prayed through the entire night" maybe three or four times, "prayed for most of the night" maybe four or five times, and "prayed long into the night" (well beyond our typical nightly prayer time) maybe 30 times or so. In other words, it hasn't been an every-night thing, but God has sought to make sure that we don't ever become too clingy to our sleep moving forward.

Currently we are in newborn-baby mode. This means we are waking up to feed baby three times a night. When we were going through this with Hudson (our firstborn) about four years ago, waking up during the night multiple times was excruciatingly difficult. But this time around, we are actually enjoying it. Eric and I get up together and make it kind of a fun time with Baby Kip and we pray together as he fills his little tummy.

When you remove self and flesh from the center of sleep, it doesn't detract from sleep—if anything, it enhances it. The two of us sleep so well when we do sleep. It's as if God has made clear to us, "When you give Me your sleep, I'll multiply and make better the sleep you do get."

We don't walk around like tired zombies during the day—in fact, we have more energy now in life than we have ever had before. It's amazing!

### Time Mismanagement

If you want to start an argument with another Christian, just tell him that God only hears prayers offered first thing in the morning. All the late nighters get really upset over the idea that true spirituality is found only in the morning.

Well, I'm not going to jump headlong into that discussion. However, I will say that whether you are a night-stalker or an early bird, *how* you handle your late nights or your early mornings is more important than *when* exactly it is that you choose to clear out your "bonus" time for prayer.

There are plenty of early risers who get up and play video games, check e-mails, read the news, and watch the latest YouTube videos. And there are plenty of late-nighters who waste their midnight hours on similar frivolities.

The key is not when you go to bed and when you wake up, but that you do it purposefully and not without thought or plan. There are only so many hours in each day, and prayer must become your fuel source. If you don't proactively rearrange your life around this all-important priority, then I can almost guarantee you that nothing is going to change.

Nighttime frittering and early morning snooze buttons must be deemed your enemies. They rob time from your King and do nothing of true value or substance with it—they just cram it in the toilet and flush. This is what I mean by mismanagement.

Eric and I have deliberately chosen to purge our lives of everything that could be classified as a time waster. Our personal time wasters weren't necessarily bad things; it's just that they were things that took time away from the more important elements of our life.

My short list: long hot baths (boy, do I love those), *Real Simple* magazine, and movies.

Eric's short list: ESPN.com, movies, and fraternizing (a little too much) down at Loodles Coffee Shop.

We both wrote our lists and then began to address them with great seriousness. We knew how significant prayer was in our lives, but we were definitely not going to be able to move forward if these personal time wasters kept hogging up our precious time.

I can honestly say that two years later I can't even fathom spending time on those things like I used to. I now enjoy a hot bath maybe once every three months; I haven't read a magazine since I can remember; and movies have become something from a different lifetime.

Eric and I have a lot on our plates, but our lives have time for prayer.

The formula is simple: Remove the time-wasters, replace them with prayer, and then be serious about protecting your newfound prayer time.

### Busyness

So much of busyness is saying yes to things you really should say no to. I realize this might be too much of an oversimplification of the solution for busyness, but I'll say it anyway: Start saying no to the things that aren't central to your life's purpose and start saying yes to the things that really matter.

Most of us have said no to prayer for so long that it feels a little awkward to say yes.

Time spent in prayer will multiply your effectiveness in the rest of your daily schedule. It's amazing, but when you prioritize the things God prioritizes, He makes sure the necessities are taken care of in your life.

Jesus did only that which His Father was doing. He wasn't a busy, frenetic person, which means His Father wasn't asking Him to do more than what was necessary. The world needs saving, but it's your business to follow God's lead and not try to tackle the problem of world hunger on your own. Take some time to prayerfully evaluate your commitments. Is there anything that is hogging up your time and focus that might not be a frivolous activity but is hindering you from real prayer? Social gatherings, parties, certain leadership roles, or overly ambitious educational and career goals often top the list of things that God might ask you to step away from, or at least reevaluate, in order to make prayer the highest priority of your life. If you come to God holding everything with an open hand, you can be sure that He will guide you and instruct you in the art of saying yes to the right things and no to the wrong ones.

### Lack of Real Desire

It's hard to pray when you don't feel like praying. But here's an important point to note: Prayer is a lot like caviar. It's an acquired taste. If you don't pray often, you won't gain a love for praying. Prayer is work, and therefore it is not very appealing to our natural sensibilities. But the simple rule of prayer is this: Begin praying, and your taste for praying will increase. The more you pray, the more you will acquire the desire for prayer, the energy for prayer, and the sense of purpose in prayer.

All things spiritual follow this same principle. God says, "Trust Me—just start doing it, and I will soon cultivate in your soul a taste for the things of My kingdom."

At times, Eric and I still battle with that sense of *blah* when we arrive at a time of prayer. But our solution isn't to say, "Well, we're both feeling blah, so I guess we shouldn't pray then." Instead, we start praying, and the first thing we start praying for is the desire, the energy, and the fire needed to pray well.

Prayer is hard work, but it is beautiful work. I want you to discover prayer as Eric and I have discovered it. It's invigorating to the soul, warming to the heart, and candy for the mind. I guess the best way to describe prayer is that it is heaven on Earth.

So don't be fooled by the blah feeling. Press onward and upward. Soon you will be dancing in the heavenly meadows of blissful intimacy with your King.

### I Don't Know How to Pray

None of us start out knowing how to pray. We are all like little babies when we start out spiritually. Babies don't even know how to eat or sleep when they start out, let alone walk, run, leap, climb, and scale El Capitan.

So the first thing we must do in the realm of prayer is accept the fact that we are infantile and we need some serious help.

And I know the best place for you to start.

Start by asking the Inventor of Prayer Himself to help. He's an excellent teacher. And even better, He is interested in not just instructing you in prayer, but in doing the praying for you. It's sort of the equivalent of not knowing how to write and asking for the spirit of Jane

Austen to come in and begin to write through you. This is how God works. He doesn't command us to go off to Prayer Seminary for six years before we can do this. Rather, He comes in and does the praying in and through us.

The next thing you can do is begin learning about prayer from those who have mastered it. Too many of us listen to others who don't have a clue about prayer and we gauge our experience accordingly. But I suggest that you turn to a few of the prayer giants of ages past and let them instruct you. Eric and I have read a lot of books on prayer, and I think the best three to start with are probably the following:

1. *Why Revival Tarries* by Leonard Ravenhill—possibly the most moving and inspiring book on prayer ever written. Eric and I have read this one loads of times.

2. *Rees Howells: Intercessor* by Norman Grubb—an amazing biography about this legendary man of prayer. Eric has read this book six or seven times.

3. *Power Through Prayer* by E.M. Bounds—Bounds has an entire library of great stuff on prayer, but this book is a great starting point.

### What if Prayer Doesn't Work?

Well, you never will know until you actually do it.

I can personally attest to the fact that not only does it work for me, but it has altered the entirety of my existence.

There have been moments when I have been served up circumstances that would challenge the notion that prayer actually works. And in those moments it would seem that the prayers I had so forcefully and faithfully prayed had somehow failed. And I heard so clearly, in those times, that syrupy whisper from the enemy: "Your God can't be trusted, can He?"

This is where Eric has been a great help to me. Eric just isn't pushed around by seeming defeat. It makes him growl all the more and believe all the more. So every time it would have seemed that our prayers had failed, Eric would say, "Let's continue to believe our God and see Him turn this around."

And that is exactly what God has done over and over again—*turned it around*. He just keeps doing it. To the point where, when Eric and I see what might look like defeat, we get excited to see how God will turn it around this time.

So much of prayer and faith is like the scene in John chapter 11, when Jesus raised Lazarus from the dead. Whereas that is one of the most profound pictures of God's power and glory being evidence on Earth, it didn't start out looking very good. Jesus was looking like an insensitive friend who didn't care enough to help. But what at first appeared like a possible slight on God's character ended up an even greater picture of His grace and glory.

## Earnestness in Prayer

This is how a prayer life works. It must learn to believe even when our personal Lazarus is stinking in a tomb for four days—believe that Jesus is the resurrection and the life and fully able to turn seeming defeat into tremendous triumph. Andrew Bonar said,

> O brother, pray; in spite of Satan, pray; spend hours in prayer; rather neglect friends than not pray; rather fast, and lose breakfast, dinner, tea, and supper—and sleep too—than not pray. And we must not talk about prayer, we must pray in right earnest. The Lord is near. He comes softly while the virgins slumber.[1]

Let's remove all the things that are keeping us from seeing our God proved strong and able in this Earth. If something is keeping you from praying, then it's keeping you and this world from knowing the power and the glory of our great God.

Here's to a radical prayer life!

# WHILE THE ENEMY SLEEPS
*following the Lamb whithersoever He goeth*

Abishai—captain over the second band of three mighties

⊰ ERIC ⊱

David was indestructible. He was untouchable. Saul did his best to destroy him, but no matter how hard he tried, only one thing was proven—David was fortressed in by the might of God. And as long as David remained under the shadow of God's wing, he was a protected life, completely impervious to the destructive forces of darkness. Second Samuel 8:6 says, "The LORD preserved David whithersoever he went."[1]

God said to Jeremiah,

> Behold, I make you this day a fortified city, an iron pillar, and bronze walls, against the whole land, against the kings of Judah, its princes, its priests, and the people of the land. They will fight against you; but they shall not prevail against you, for I am with you, says the LORD, to deliver you (Jeremiah 1:18-19 RSV).

In addition to Jeremiah, this was the reality of David. This was the reality of David's Mighties. This was the reality of Jesus. And this was the reality of every one of Jesus' Mighties who have walked this earth over the past 2000 years.

They were untouchable. The enemy targeted them with every last gun he possessed but they were impervious, at the soul level, to his schemes.

First Peter 3:13 declares, "Who is he that will harm you, if ye be followers of that which is good?"

The Mighties are men and women who suffer great physical pains, but the Mighties are never killed by the enemy. Rather, they offer their body and blood to be spent for the cause of their Christ and for the purposes of His glory. Mighties don't die random deaths, but martyrs' deaths. Their body and their blood is expended strategically and never randomly. Their God holds their life as precious and He sets His angels at guard about them lest they dash their foot against a stone.

God's Gibborim cannot be taken by the enemy; rather, they willingly give themselves up. The heroes of Christ covenant with their King, knowing that they will walk this Earth like immortals until the day God says, "Now, will you be spent for Me?"

Jesus said to His Company of Heroes in Luke 10:19, "Behold, I give unto you power to tread on serpents and scorpions, and over all the power of the enemy: and nothing shall by any means hurt you."

The apostle Paul was shipwrecked, scourged, beaten, stoned, and imprisoned. Men covenanted on their life to kill him, but his life was preserved though storms threatened, rocks battered his head and body, and blood gushed from his skin.

One time, Paul lay as if dead upon the ground outside the city of Lystra. He was stoned by an angry mob and tossed outside the gates of the city as if he were trash. But it wasn't yet Paul's time, and he rose back to life and stormed right back into Lystra with a spiritual swagger reminiscent of King David's.

Another time Paul was bitten by a deadly viper, but instead of panicking he merely tossed the poisonous snake into a fire and "felt no harm" (Acts 28:5).

Paul was strong, undeniable, impervious, and seemingly immortal until his earthly race was finished and God whispered to him, "It's time, My dear son! It's time to be spent!"

We read of Job that he was surrounded by a hedge of protection.

It was a hedge that Satan couldn't pass through. It is this very same hedge that surrounds God's Gibborim. It is a boundary of blood that preserves those of us who enter into the covenant graces of our Jesus. It is a boundary that darkness cannot pass unless we allow it to, unless we yield to its cunning requests for entry.

Yes, as it says in Hebrews chapter 11, the Mighties throughout history were stoned, sawn asunder, tempted, slain with the sword. They wandered about in sheepskins and goatskins, being destitute, afflicted, tormented. But this great cloud of witnesses who have gone before us chose to confirm their King no matter the cost to their physical bodies. They picked up their crosses and followed their King, knowing that their seemingly pitiable expenditure of life was no meaningless travesty, but the glory of God made manifest through loving, sacrificial devotion.

There is a statement in Revelation chapter 14 that never ceases to move me: "These are they which follow the Lamb whithersoever he goeth" (verse 4).

The Mighties follow the Lamb no matter where He goes. They trust that should they be in front of an angry mob that they will rest secure in His sovereign grip; should they be before kings and princes that they will stand and speak with the utterance given them by the Spirit; and should they be up the Via Dolorosa, up to Golgotha carrying a heavy cross, dripping with blood, and enduring the cruel taunts of the enemy that, even in such a scene, the grace and strength of their King will guide them and supply them with everything they need for victory.

The Mighties are certain in their untouchability.

As Paul wrote,

> Who shall separate us from the love of Christ? shall tribulation, or distress, or persecution, or famine, or nakedness, or peril, or sword?...Nay, in all these things we are more than conquerors through him that loved us (Romans 8:35,37).

This is invincibility! A deep soul knowledge that nothing—whether it be a cross, the gallows, the guillotine, or the stake—can defeat us.

It's knowing that nothing can rob us of the ultimate victory and nothing can turn our loyalties from our King.

There is a story in the book of 1 Samuel that demonstrates this extraordinary "knowing." David looked over at two of his warriors and proposed the most outrageous thing. At the time Saul was on a witch hunt for David, and David was on the run. But lo and behold, David and his men stumbled across Saul's camp. And there was Saul, sleeping in the midst of his strong men.

An ordinary man would have run for his life. But David was no ordinary man. He was an untouchable born of the Spirit of the Almighty. David was a miracle man, graced with a wall of bronze about him. So, in seeing Saul and his strongest men asleep, he said to Ahimelech and to Abishai, "Who will go down with me to Saul to the camp?" (26:6).

Was David crazy? To walk in amongst Saul's armies while they slept was suicide!

Ahimelech was silent, but Abishai responded, "I will go down with thee."

"These are they which follow the Lamb whithersoever he goeth."

Read the Bible afresh and you will be forced to admit that what Jesus proposes for His Mighties is no less crazy than what David was proposing to his.

But David didn't force his men to follow. He asked them simply, "Who will go down with me?"

Jesus doesn't force His followers either. Rather, He appeals to them and says, "Who will follow Me?"

David and Abishai walked straight into the camp of the enemy while they slept. Scripture says that God put Saul and his men into a deep slumber. And David and Abishai mocked the power of Saul by grabbing his spear as well as removing a cruse of water from his satchel and sneaking off with it in the night.

To follow Jesus is to follow an untouchable. To stay close at His side is to know that even in the midst of the most hostile territory God can make the enemy fall into a deep slumber.

But will you go on this outrageous mission when your King asks?

You do have a choice.

Ahimelech remained silent, watching the drama from a safe distance. But Abishai craved the nearness of his beloved commander and eagerly took up the charge and followed his king into the bowels of the enemy.

"These are they which follow the Lamb whithersoever he goeth."

Your King Jesus is just as seemingly reckless as that freshly anointed shepherd boy named David. He is unafraid of walking into the temple with a whip and clearing out the money changers. He is unabashed about loving the unlovables and touching the social outcasts. He is unashamed of hanging on a tree and being perceived as a common criminal if that is where His Father directs His steps.

Our Jesus' actions may be termed brash and headstrong by some. Others may claim Him to be arrogant for standing against the religious leaders of His day rather than submitting to their wisdom and authority. But Jesus wasn't haughty or proud. He was confident—confident in His God, in His position, in the truth, and in His untouchability.

And our King desires to breed this soul confidence in each of His men and women. He desires to train them to follow without question, heed command without hesitation, and climb up on crosses and die without reticence when the opportunity presents itself.

This world is full of Ahimelechs. Nearly every man on Earth hesitates when Jesus says, "Who will go with Me?" But I challenge you to become an Abishai and gain a name among the Mighties. Ahimelech might escape the situation unscathed, but Abishai left that night knowing that his king had power over all his enemies.

You may acknowledge intellectually that your King has power over all His enemies, but the only way that you will *know* this truth intimately in the depths of your soul is if you follow Him into the camp of the enemy and witness this power for yourself.

# *a moment for prayer*
## AUDACITY

⊰ LESLIE ⊱

I know I've thrown a lot of principles at you in this book; however, at risk of sounding a bit too much like a Chinese proverb, I have one more to share:

*The more audacity in the prayer, the better.*

Elephants like peanuts, monkeys like bananas, bees like pollen, and mice like cheese. These are facts we all know from a young age. But very few of us ever learned, when we were five years old, that God likes audacity.

Our God seems to love the notion of His children asking big—*really* big. Go throughout the Bible and you see this audacity thing everywhere you turn.

## Audicious Moments in Scripture

Eric and I have compiled a "top-sixteen audacious moments in Scripture list." I've adapted this from one of Eric's blogposts from late 2008:

### *Audacious Moment #16*

Peter commanding a man who has withered legs to stand up and start walking.

### *Audacious Moment #15*

Jashobeam, the Tachmonite, fighting off 800 Philistines all by his lonesome.

*Audacious Moment #14*

King Josiah romping through the land of Israel turning to dust anything and everything that was an abomination to his God.

*Audacious Moment #13*

Elijah picking a fight with 450 prophets of Baal on Mount Carmel. Digging a trench about the altar and pouring in 12 barrels of water (4 barrels x 3 times) wasn't exactly sane either.

*Audacious Moment #12*

Three of David's mightiest men break through the Philistine garrison in Bethlehem and fight off a horde of indignant Philistines—all to grab a mere cup of cool water from the well at Bethlehem for their king.

*Audacious Moment #11*

Paul, after being smashed to death with stones by the people of Lystra, rises back to life and heads straight back to the very people that had just stoned him.

*Audacious Moment #10*

Caleb, at 85 years of age, claiming Hebron, the mountain of the giants, as his inheritance in the Land of Promise. Not only did he want it (which is audacious enough), but he personally led the battle formation that climbed the mountain and destroyed the giant men who lived there.

*Audacious Moment #9*

Samson picking a fight with 1000 Philistines and using a donkey's jawbone to destroy every last one of them.

*Audacious Moment #8*

Joab climbing up the gutter of Jebus ahead of all David's troops and being the first to jump in amongst a throng of enemy soldiers and strike the mocking Jebusites on the cheek in order to defend the honor of his king.

### Audacious Moment #7

Elisha, when told by the mighty prophet Elijah to ask for anything and it shall be done, asks for a double portion of the power and anointing of Elijah. I love it!

### Audacious Moment #6

David, while still a youngster, running after a lion while it has a lamb in its mouth. He grabbed its mane, broke its jaw, and gained back his lamb.

### Audacious Moment #5

Benaiah jumping into a pit with a lion on a snowy day and killing the riled beast.

### Audacious Moment #4

David and Abishai sneaking into the camp of Saul at night while he was surrounded by his mightiest warriors and brashly stealing his spear and water cruse. That's not just audacious, that's hilarious!

### Audacious Moment #3

David going into hand-to-hand combat with Goliath, the greatest warrior of his generation, without armor and without a sword. And he doesn't enter the fray with sheepish anxiety; he sprints with ferocity at this man-beast and kills him in a matter of seconds. Most of us don't realize how truly amazing this scene was.

### Audacious Moment #2

Jesus deliberately choosing to stay away from Bethany until Lazarus had not only died but had been rotting in the tomb for four days. Not until then does He show up and He has the guts to say, "Roll away the stone. Lazarus, come forth!"

## *Audacious Moment #1*

God, in open mockery of the power of darkness, sends forth His Son into hostile enemy territory as a helpless little baby. God defeats sin, death, and Satan while gagged, bound, stripped naked, and nailed to two pieces of wood. The entirety of the gospel is the audacity of God to die a criminal's death and openly mock the powers of this world as a helpless little lamb of sacrifice. It's truly amazing!

## Audacious Asking

What areas of prayer is God asking you to be audacious in? When Eric was in college, God challenged him to begin praying every day for his future wife. Then he had a thought: *I bet no other guys out there are praying for their future wives. That means I can be really bold in what I'm asking for—I don't have any competition!* So he started praying, "God, bring me the most pure-hearted, faithful, and beautiful woman on the planet!" Eric declares that God answered his prayer— though I certainly feel very unworthy of such a statement! Whether or not *I* feel that I fit the description of the "most pure-hearted, faithful, and beautiful," the important thing is that from Eric's perspective, God answered his bold request with perfect faithfulness. The "future wife" prayer was Eric's first attempt at praying audaciously. It helped set the stage for many more outlandishly big requests in our lives that we've seen God answer.

Eric and I feel that we have only just begun to experience the heights and depths of wrestling, importunate prayer. We fully expect to continue learning and growing in this area for the rest of our lives. But one thing I can say for certain is that I have never seen so much answered prayer in my life since devoting myself two years ago to continual fervent, specific, bold praying.

When we found out that the process of adopting a baby from Korea would probably take six to eight months (normally it takes two years, but because she was a "waiting child" with special needs, the process was faster), I began to pray daily that her case would be the fastest one our agency had ever processed. This was a rather audacious request, since the agency had literally done thousands of adoptions. But soon, miracles began to happen left and right. Government forms that normally took ten weeks were processed in seven days. Paperwork that usually takes months sailed through the red tape. When we got the call saying that the baby was ready to be picked up from Korea after *less than three months*, the people at the agency said, "This has to be the fastest adoption our agency has ever done!" There was no explanation other than the supernatural power of God. Out of thousands of adoptions, ours was the fastest ever. Why? Because we laid a bold, specific request before our Lord, and He faithfully answered.

Even more miraculous was the provision of money for her adoption. After we made the decision to pursue her, we learned we needed to come up with $15,535 in a matter of three weeks. We had no idea where the money would come from—so we prayed boldly and specifically. And the very day we were required to write the check, we had received a miraculous provision of exactly $15,535—down to the very dollar. Harper's adoption is just one of the many incredible miracles we've seen since we began building our lives around prayer.

Ephesians 3:20 says that God is able to do exceedingly abundantly beyond all we can ask or think—so we might as well ask big. Of course, like we said before, we must pray "God prayers" in order to see our audacious requests granted. Praying audaciously for selfish wants and pleasures won't yield miraculous results, but praying the prayers that are on our King's heart always will.

Corrie ten Boom once wrote about being in a hotel in Russia and seeing a downcast cleaning woman. Corrie felt a heavy burden to reach her for Christ, but when she tried to approach her with a tract, the woman gave her a dirty look and shooed her away. Disappointed, Corrie walked into an elevator and began to pray. "Lord, I claim this woman's soul for Your kingdom." Then she hesitated. Was it right for her to pray such a bold prayer? But she felt sure that God wanted her to stand in faith for the woman's salvation. Soon, she found herself taking it a step further. "Lord, I claim all of Russia for Your kingdom!" About a half hour later, Corrie was in her hotel room, and the cleaning woman knocked at the door. Surprised, Corrie let her in the room. It didn't take long before she realized that the woman was asking for a tract. When Corrie handed it to her, the woman's face expressed joy, and she hugged Corrie in heartfelt gratitude. Corrie knew that her prayer of faith was yielding eternal fruit and that God was blessing her audacious asking.[1]

Another time, Corrie was in a men's prison in Africa. The men were hopeless, depressed, and miserable—sitting in mud and filth, their eyes devoid of any life. They didn't seem interested as she began talking to them about Jesus. Corrie prayed and said, "Lord, I claim Your promise of joy. Flood this prison with unspeakable joy right now!" Within a few minutes, the men had come alive. Their faces were radiant and excited. They began to listen to her message of salvation and hope. They leaned forward, eagerly drinking in all that she shared. And then they began to celebrate. In the midst of darkness, they had found life. In the midst of death, they had found a reason to live again. As she drove away, the prisoners surrounded her car and called out, "Old woman! Come back again and tell us more about Jesus!" This was another example of God honoring audacious faith.[2]

Think of the most challenging prayer requests in your life—a health issue, a financial issue, salvation for a wayward loved one, etc. Rather than sheepishly muttering a few half-hopeful, half-doubting prayers about that issue, begin praying bold, audacious prayers and watch what God does. For example, don't merely pray, "Lord, bring my drug-addict younger brother to salvation and help him clean up his life." Rather, pray along the lines of, "Lord, bring my brother into Your kingdom and make him one of the mightiest spiritual warriors who has ever lived. Bring millions into Your kingdom through his testimony."

That might sound larger-than-life—but remember, God is able to do exceedingly, abundantly beyond all we could *ask or think*. When we pray the things that are on our King's heart, no matter how outlandishly audacious your prayers might sound to your own ears, they are nothing in light of God's willingness and ability to answer.

# THE CAVE OF ADULLAM
*the secret place of the king*

❧ ERIC ❧

I magine what our world would be like today if even one of the great and mighty men of the Bible were alive today.

Imagine the spiritual swagger of David dressed in modern garb. Imagine the loving and unquestioning devotion of Joab injected into today's Christian world. Imagine the daring and the wisdom of Jashobeam walking into the dens of darkness and single-handedly setting captives free. Imagine the tenacity of Eleazar and Shammah infused into the corridors of the present-day church. And imagine the purity, the loyalty, and the might of Benaiah coursing through the veins of a modern-day prophet.

Is the stuff of the Mighties the stuff of fiction? Is the content of these men's lives just the exaggerations of poets and the unfettered imaginings of silly girls? Or is this stuff real?

Could it be that the stuff of the Mighties is meant to be the stuff of today's believers? Could it be that, though it seems preposterous and cartoonish in its scope and grandeur, that the Gibborim of God are merely the by-product of a common man's givenness to his King?

Leslie and I believe that with all of our hearts, souls, minds, and strength.

This superhuman stuff is yours for the taking. But, as I said in the beginning, only those who possess a five-year-old's heart will take it.

You and I have entered into the sacred chamber of our King through the pages of this book. We are awed by His power, awed by His glory, and we find ourselves kneeling in adoration before His regal throne.

He is saying to each of us, "If you want this, then I will give it to you!"

But there is a part of each of us that hesitates to reach out and accept this.

Why would we hesitate even for a moment?

We hesitate because we instinctively know that life will have to forever change if we seize this opportunity. We know that we will never be able to go back to our days of selfish and fleshly ignorance. We are aware of the fact that we are not just gaining something great, but we are losing something in this transaction.

What is it we are losing?

We are losing the controls of our life. And, to be quite frank, we like being in control.

We are giving up the comforts of our life. Because to be one of the Mighties means that you follow your King wherever He goes, no matter if your head rests on a rock or on a pillow at night. And, honestly, we prefer the predictability and the coziness of our pillows.

We are giving up the confidence in our self, our abilities, our intellect, our wisdom, and our might. And we know that once we do that, the credit for our life's success will no longer be able to flow back toward us. It will be God who gets the glory, and we secretly love to have that glory for ourselves.

We are giving up all the excuses that we have concocted over the years for living a mediocre and marginal existence. For the moment that we take on the power, the might, and the majesty of Christ is the moment that everything mediocre and everything marginal in our existence is exposed and forced to leave.

And if that was not enough reason to hold back from taking this extraordinary gift, there is also the fact that we know that once we make this exchange, our precious reputation will be shot. We will forever be classified as "one of those," and the world's impression of us will certainly become tainted and warped. For if we follow Christ, we are guaranteed to have His enemies become our enemies.

An angel of God presented the apostle John with a little book. And the angel said, "Take it, and eat it" (Revelation 10:9).

What an odd request.

But the angel added a little caveat to his request: "The words of the book will taste like honey in your mouth, John, but they will be bitter and hard when it comes to digestion and working it through your inner man."

And sure enough, when John ate the words, they were honey-sweet in his mouth and then suddenly the reality of these words dawned upon his stomach and he felt the uncomfortable churning in his digestive tract.

It's very possible that the sweet- and noble-sounding words of this book are beginning to make their way down to your stomach. The idea of becoming a Mighty resonates with the deepest part of our being as men and women, but the cost of becoming a Mighty is more than most are willing to pay. And that is precisely why there are very few Mighties in every generation.

Let's admit it—we want to be named amongst the Most Mighty, but we don't want to have to leave everything we know and love to follow our King into the wilderness of obscurity.

Jesus said, "Unless you eat the flesh of the Son of Man and drink His blood, you have no life in you" (John 6:53 NKJV).

This statement ranks right up there with the one the angel spoke to John about eating that little book. It's odd.

But this statement is what this whole book is about. We must partake of Jesus. We must allow the reality, the very person of our King to enter into our bodies and overtake us, rule us, and love us. He must become our life, our strength, our passion, our purpose.

It sounds great to say that the Most Mighty Man of all time wishes to give you His might, His valor, His courage, and His supernatural power as a gift.

Who would turn such a gift down?

But then we hear the catch. Not only do we get His power but we get His persecution. Not only do we get His health and wholeness, but we also get His homelessness and shame. Yes, we receive His strength, but we also share in His sufferings. We share in His riches at the same time we share in His disparaged reputation and His revilement.

And unless we partake of our King—every part of Him—unless we are willing to leave everything for His sake, unless we are ready to follow Him to the cross and die right beside Him in shame, we can have no part with Him.

It tastes honey-sweet in the mouth, but this little book (known as the Word of God) is a doozy to digest.

Scripture says of the disciples who surrounded Jesus that when Jesus gave the ultimatum and clarified what it really took to follow Him, that "from that time many of his disciples went back, and walked no more with him."

What are you going to do?

This is everything you desire, everything you want. But are you willing to forsake everything you know and love to get it? Are you willing to give up the controls of your life, the comforts of your life, the applause you have grown to love, and relinquish that precious reputation?

The Mighties have all come to this place of decision. They have all been presented with the little book and been told to eat. And the one striking similarity amongst the multitude of God's Gibborim through all the ages is that each and every one of God's true follow- ers ate the little book—they all, each and every one of them, partook of their King's life.

Giving up life as you now know it is a scary proposition. But this is the uncomfortable process by which God's heroes are shaped.

King David is in hiding. His very integrity is challenged in the highest seats of authority in Israel. Who will stand with the rightful king of Israel?

Joab heard of David's plight. He fully understood what it would mean to stand with this young man. It would mean leaving everything he knew and loved behind. It would mean a deliberate rebellion against the man currently wearing the crown in Israel and thus the entire armed forces of Saul being set against him.

Jashobeam heard of David's situation. He too knew good and well what it would cost him to confirm this young man as king of Israel. He knew that his body and blood would be required of him.

And don't think for a moment that Eleazar, Shammah, Benaiah, and Abishai didn't know that their king's situation and reputation wouldn't immediately become their own the moment that they joined him and covenanted in the bond of blood with him.

These were not stupid men. They were the wisest of men, the most courageous of men. These were men who partook of their king's life to the fullest measure. They partook of his ignominy, and therefore they were worthy to partake of his glory.

What will you do when you hear of your King's situation? When you hear that He is hiding in the Cave of Adullam, will you say to your neighbor, "I'm voting for David in the next election"? Or will you actually get off your keister, go to where your King is, and offer Him your life?

God isn't looking for votes, He is looking for lives. He's not interested in His popularity rating amongst the rank-and-file Israelites, He is interested in finding out who is "all in"!

When He looks about Himself today in the Cave of Adullam, will He see you standing there?

"Who is this new recruit?" the King might say.

Joab might take you by the shoulder and say, "He longs to join Your band, Highness."

"Is he proven?" Jashobeam might ask.

"Is he loyal?" Benaiah might bark.

"Bring him here!" the King might say. "He is risking life and limb to even be here with us now—for Me that is enough."

"But will he run when the battle turns fierce?" Eleazar might question.

"You were all common men when you first met Me in this cave," the King might respond. "And it was I who shared with you My swagger and My strength. So do not look down your noses upon such a young believer—for if he is willing, I will make him to be numbered amongst the most mighty ones to ever live."

The Cave of Adullam is not far away in distance, but it is supremely difficult to reach through the vast thicket of our flesh.

There are millions of men and women who esteem Jesus Christ as the rightful King of this world, but only a small band of them who truly do leave everything, brave the winds of persecution and infamy, and labor to see this King crowned and anointed as such in this natural world.

The Cave of Adullam is a fearful place to many. It's the place of the hunted, the place of the despised, the place of the outlawed, the place of suffering. And yet, though most are distracted by the fact that this cave boasts the strongest concentration of rebels, and therefore is the enemy's most sought-after target—it is also the place of the King.

To the Mighties, the Cave of Adullam is anything but a fearful place. For this is the place where their King rests His head. It is the place of divine stratagem, the congregating center for the heroes of the kingdom. It is the place of intimate communion, the place of secrets, the place of command, and the place of commission.

To the Mighties, it is an honor to enter into David's hidden sanctuary. For the Mighties it is their great privilege to know the secret whereabouts of their beloved ruler.

The Mighties, back in the age of David, referred to this sacred cave as "the rock." It was a hidden place, yes, but it was the source of their strength. For after every battle, they would return there, to their king's presence, and there they would find an overwhelming sense of security and grace. It is in "the rock" that they would receive their confidence and their assurance of victory. It is in "the rock" that these men would be renewed and reinvigorated in their spiritual swagger.

One of the most beautiful, majestic, and awe-inspiring stories of the Mighties took place in this very cave. Scripture says that David's three mightiest men came down to him in the Cave of Adullam. And it was in this most intimate place of secrets that these three overheard their king express his deepest longing.

The Philistine armies had claimed David's hometown of Bethlehem. The birthplace of the Mighties was being held hostage by David's enemy. David was astir with emotion. And these three closest were there to overhear his most intimate thoughts.

We read that David said, "Oh that one would give me drink of the water of the well of Bethlehem, which is by the gate!" (2 Samuel 23:15).

Who was able to hear this intimate desire of the king expressed? Who was able to discern this heartfelt longing?

Those outside the cave could not hear it. Those outside "the rock" could not discern this most intimate yearning of their king's heart. It was private, it was secret—but it was made available to these three who had risked everything to meet their king in his sanctuary of suffering.

We read that these three Mighties immediately embarked upon the most heedless, most daring mission maybe in all military history. They were so intimate with their king, and they adored their king so desperately, that when they heard this secret longing of his heart, they, as a band of reckless love-soldiers, broke through the garrison of the Philistine army, fought off all resistance, took a cup full of water from the well of Bethlehem, and then heroically fought their way back to the hidden sanctuary of their beloved.

These men stormed the gates of hell for love itself. They considered not the impossibility of such a venture. They didn't ponder the fact that three men diving headlong into the very bosom of enemy power cannot possibly make it back out alive.

These were men who were moved, motivated, and carried on the wings of absolute devotion. These were men who slept next to their beloved in the sanctuary of suffering. They were made "rocks" by communing with their beloved in "the rock." Their bodies were for their king to break; their blood was for their king to shed.

When these three Mighties returned with their sacred booty, David would not drink of it. Rather, he poured the water out to the Lord. And he said, "Be it far from me, O LORD, that I should do this: is not this the blood of the men that went in jeopardy of their lives?" (verse 17).

What a beautiful scene! What love! What devotion from men to king, and from king back to men!

The king looked at his men with tears streaming down his cheeks. He saw in their eyes the passion, the love, and the utter surrender to his existence. He saw the fresh blood of battle splattered all over their faces and dripping from their swords. And he was presented with a cup of water from the well of Bethlehem. They had given him his heart's desire.

But no matter the treasure that water may have represented in David's heart, and no matter the pleasure David may have felt in drinking that sacred water from his birthplace—*he treasured his men more.* His greatest pleasure was not in this cup of water, but in the hearts of his valiant men.

Every one of us is invited to the Cave of Adullam. Every one of us is welcome to be partakers of our King's most intimate thoughts and desires. Every one of us is privileged to lay our head where our King lays His. But, oh how few there are who choose to truly share in His sufferings.

The apostle Paul wrote, "As we share abundantly in Christ's sufferings, so through Christ we share abundantly in comfort too" (2 Corinthians 1:5 RSV).

The Mighties tasted something that the rest of us who refuse to share in our King's sufferings can never taste. Paul said that he was happy to share in the sufferings of his King, because in doing so, he was also able to share in the intimate comfort, the intimate consolation, refreshment, and encouragement of his beloved Jesus.

We so often keep at a distance from this cave of secrets, thinking we are choosing a better, more satisfying life, when in actuality we are removing ourselves from the truest, most perfect life—the life of our King.

Paul spoke the motto of every Mighty down through the ages; he gave the true motivation of every God-built man down through the centuries. He said, it's "that I may know him, and the power of his resurrection, and the fellowship of his sufferings, being made conformable unto his death" (Philippians 3:10).

This is a motivation that is wholly foreign to our modern Christian sensibilities. Paul was saying, "Do you want to know why I have spent my life with my King in this sanctuary of suffering? I'll tell you! It's so that I may fully know Him, partake of His spiritual swagger, sympathize with Him in His hiding, and truly be made like Him in His amazing life of heroic sacrifice!"

Does Christ's cave scare you, or do you find yourself strangely drawn? Do you despise such worldly derision, or are you fascinated to know the intimate presence of your King? Are you wanting to support Jesus from a distance, or are you willing to support Him as one of His adoring, devoted soldiers?

Many applauded Jesus from a distance as He walked this Earth, but only a small band of soldiers stood by Him all the way through until His ascension. There were only 120 who congregated in the upper room, awaiting the outpouring of His mighty power in Jerusalem.

Are you the stuff of the multitudes, or are you the stuff of the few?

Our Jesus has single-handedly broken through the Philistine garrison in Bethlehem in order to bring us a cup of cold water for our thirsty souls. And He did this with the hands of His deity tied behind His back. He did this mighty feat as a baby. He proved that His "weakness" is still infinitely more powerful than the enemy's greatest strength. As the Lamb He roundly defeated the roaring lions of sin and death. And He has come to each of us, drenched in His own blood, bearing in His crimson-stained hands a cup of cold water. And this water is living water; this water is His life.

David poured out the water given him by the Mighties. But Jesus says to you, "You must drink it to live!"

Our Jesus has proven His valor, He has proven His great love, and here He stands with nail wounds in His hands and feet and an open spear wound in His side, saying, "Will you partake of Me? Will you come to My cave and know Me? Will you rest your head where I rest Mine? Will you allow Me to make you likened unto Myself? Will you allow Me to make you mighty? Will you allow Me to implant My spiritual swagger inside your believing heart?"

Jesus doesn't need men and women who merely *esteem* Him as great, but believers who are willing to be *made* great by His life.

Jesus isn't looking for men and women who merely agree with His gospel, but believers who are willing to flesh out and actually live His gospel in their daily lives.

Jesus isn't looking for men and women who merely know about His Mighty warriors of old, but rather He is in search of men and women who are willing to be fashioned after their very same pattern by the almighty kingly Potter of Souls.

If your reputation is so important to you that you are unwilling to leave everything for the secret cave of Jesus, then you are unworthy to call yourself by His sacred name.

If your comforts are too precious to you that you are unable to relinquish them in exchange for His life, then you are unworthy to call yourself by His sacred name.

If you allow your ambition, your intellect, your wealth, your abilities, your lusts, or your fears to restrain you from offering yourself wholly and completely to your Commander, then you are unworthy to call yourself by His sacred name.

The name of Jesus is too precious to be spent on those who denigrate it with their attempts to integrate it with their selfish existence. The name of Jesus is for those who are unashamed of His cave and who venture there to join the fellowship of the burning hearts.

His cave is where I'll be. I dearly hope that I see you there!

# a moment for prayer
## IMMOVABLE

❧ LESLIE ❧

Leonard Ravenhill wrote, "Men of prayer must be men of steel, for they will be assaulted by Satan even before they attempt to assault his kingdom."[1]

When you begin to take steps forward in wrestling prayer, you can bank on the fact that the enemy will pull out all the stops to try to thwart and discourage you. As Amy Carmichael said,

> Our enemy is more aware than we are of the spiritual possibilities that depend upon obedience. We should never be surprised that he seeks by assault and, if that fails, by undermining our defenses, to compel us to give way.[2]

When Nehemiah was in the process of building the wall around Jerusalem, the enemies of Israel did everything possible to thwart the construction work:

> When Sanballat, Tobiah, the Arabs, the Ammonites, and the Ashdodites heard that the walls of Jerusalem were being restored and the gaps were beginning to be closed…they became very angry, and all of them conspired together to come and attack Jerusalem and create confusion (Nehemiah 4:7-8 NKJV).

What an incredible picture of the enemy's tactic against us! Whenever we move forward in prayer, he does everything he can to create confusion. Using doubt, discouragement, or fear, he creates a "smoke and mirrors" magic show of illusion, trying to make himself appear more powerful than he really is, trying to convince us that we will never succeed in completing the building process.

If you find that you are being constantly distracted by the cares of life, bogged down with emotional or physical "fog," or pestered with irrational thoughts and fears every time you try to pray, there is a good chance that the enemy of your soul is attempting to create confusion and keep you from entering the cave with your King. Beware of saying, "I'll press into God once these issues are gone." That's exactly how the enemy wants you to respond. Like Nehemiah, we must aggressively pray and fight until the enemy realizes that we will not kowtow to his bullying.

Listen to Nehemiah:

> Nevertheless we made our prayer to our God, and because of them we set a watch against them day and night…Therefore I positioned men behind the lower parts of the wall, at the openings; and I set the people according to their families, with their swords, their spears, and their bows. And I looked, and arose and said to the nobles, to the leaders, and to the rest of the people, "Do not be afraid of them. Remember the Lord, great and awesome, and fight…And it happened, when our enemies heard that it was known to us, and that God had brought their plot to nothing, that all of us returned to the wall, everyone to his work (Nehemiah 4:9-15 NKJV).

Christ said, "Watch and pray, lest you enter into temptation" (Matthew 26:41 NKJV).

If you remain constantly on guard against the enemy, setting "a watch upon your wall," and fight aggressively in prayer against all attack and confusion, then the enemy's plots will amount to absolutely nothing. Soon, you will be shaped into one of God's Mighties and you will become *offensive*, rather than defensive, in the spiritual realm.

Stay on guard against the tactics of the enemy. And remember, all we need to do is resist the devil, and he *must* flee (see James 4:7).

13

# The Victory Dance
*becoming undignified for our Lord*

⊰ Eric ⊱

So what really are God's expectations of the believing life? That is the question posed in this book.

I propose that a truly godly hero, built after the pattern of heaven and not the pattern of this culture, is something altogether "other" than what we see today in and amongst Christian leadership.

A truly consecrated life takes no thought for the self but is radically abandoned to the purposes of the King.

A radically covenanted believer is ferocious and tenacious for the glory of her beloved Christ, and she will happily risk body and blood to confirm Jesus as the rightful King of this universe.

A truly godly hero is built after the pattern of the Mighties, the pattern of the Word of God Himself—he is fashioned after the gritty, flesh-diminishing truth of Scripture and imbued with the love of heaven and carried into battle on the wings of utter devotion.

A loyalist to the High King of heaven possesses the spiritual swagger of the freshly anointed. She knows her untouchability and her invincibility in Christ and thus holds the necks of lions, bears, and giants firmly in her hands and under her sway.

A heroic man is pure in his heart and mind and perfectly loyal in his innermost being to the purposes of Christ's kingdom.

A heroic woman is not her own, but lives out the life of another—the purposes, the plans, the behavior, the love of one much greater than herself.

A heroic man is unashamed of bearing the nature, the cause, the piercing message, and the awful stigma of his Lord.

A heroic woman is born in Bethlehem, communes and grows up in the Cave of Adullam, and then enters Jerusalem in utter humility to bear the cross of her dear Adonai.

Are you a devotee?

Does such a list of qualifiers cause you grief, or does it stir desire in you?

I am not yet of the rank and remembrance of God's Gibborim, and yet such a list moves me; it causes my heart to yearn with longing. I want it, and I want it all. I want my King's stigma! I want my King's shame! I want my King's sufferings! Because I want my King's closeness! I want my dear Captain's comfort! I want to know Him not merely in name, but in intimate discourse. And I will give up everything for such a privilege!

This book has been written in a coffee shop, but as we've been talking, I have completely forgotten my cup of chai tea sitting inches from my hand. I've been miles away exploring the hills and heather of Judea. I have been searching the town of Bethlehem to see if there are others willing to be born of this ancient bloodline of might. I have been laying my head upon a rock in the depths of the Cave of Adullam and gazing lovingly into the face of my beloved Commander and Chief. And I have been spying out the streets of Jerusalem, asking my Lord to prepare me to walk this dusty way with a cross upon my shoulder.

I have forgotten that there are others bustling about us here at Loodles. I have lost myself in the simple desire that you might feel the full weight of our King's call upon your soul. You may be the only one who reaches this page in the book. You may be the only one with enough spiritual guts to keep going when the requirements of our Christ amplify up to their full and rightful volume.

I realize that it might seem strange to you that this message might have been written and fashioned just for you. But you must choose to receive it as such. It is the personal commission of the King of the universe *to you*.

It's possible that no one else will follow. Every other man and woman who entered this conversation may end up choosing to despise it. But I pray that you won't follow the multitudes, and instead, you will allow God to woo you into the fold of the few.

I said in the very beginning that it is my desire that our generation would gain a name amongst the two most mighty generations of all time. But I challenge you to seek admittance into God's Gibborim even if you are the only one. Even if, God forbid, I were to grow lax in this battle and drop my sword, you must never. Keep your eyes focused on your King and on no man.

David was more than Mighty, he was more than God's champion. David was a man unashamed of his God. He was a man who was more than a conqueror—he was also a worshipper, an adorer of his Jehovah.

Today's men often shy away from singing songs of love. We shy away from dancing out of sheer delight. But David was the premier man, and he sang and danced to the point of becoming undignified for his beloved.

All too many of us shout when our team scores, but we are silent when our God triumphs.

As the story goes, the Ark of Covenant finally arrived at Jerusalem. And as it entered into the bosom of that great city, David was filled with such exuberance, such euphoria that he removed his clothing and danced about in the streets of the sacred capital with nothing more than a loincloth wrapped about his waist. This was a priceless historic occasion. The Spirit of the Almighty was entering into David's dwelling place. It was a picture of Pentecost thousands of years before the second chapter of Acts unfolded in like manner upon the very same streets.

Scripture says that David was a man after God's own heart. He knew the significance of such a thing as the presence of God entering into the heart of Israel. And whereas other men may not have understood and appreciated the incoming of the power of God into the breast of God's people, David knew this was the gospel.

And David danced.

Are you willing to dance?

And he danced in a loincloth. He was willing to look the fool before all Israel to express to his God his utter devotion. He was despised for it, but he refused to hold back in his effusive worship.

Jesus hung naked.

Are you willing to hang naked on a tree before a mocking, reviling crowd of beastly humanity?

Jesus, the Most Mighty of all, was willing to appear weak, wrong, and defeated in order to express His love to His Father and to each of us. History tells us that...

- Peter was crucified upside down after telling his murderers that he was unworthy of dying as his King died.

- Andrew was publicly tied to two beams of wood and left to hang dying for three days.

- James was thrown from the top of the temple and killed upon the very same streets that David danced.

- Paul was beheaded.

- John was submerged into a pot of boiling oil and then was exiled to the island of Patmos.

And Scripture records that Stephen was crushed with stones.

The Mighties are the reviled ones—they always have been. And they are not deterred for even a moment from receiving the same disdain that their King received and still receives.

The Mighties are not so proud that they are unwilling to be stripped of all dignity in order to bear the full weight of their King's suffering. They are not preservers of personal reputation, but rather, preservers of the glory of their Beloved. They are, each and every one of them, willing to become an outlaw in this world if they can be accepted into the intimate honor roll of their precious Master.

The Mighties are men who die willingly, and they die with a song issuing from their hearts. They are not cowardly to shout at the top of their lungs in the streets of Jerusalem, "Jesus is my King!"

Jesus is looking for a few good heroes.

Who will be this generation's Joab? Who will be the first to rush upon Jebus and strike the cheek of the enemy? Who will be bold enough to risk life and limb in order to secure Jerusalem for their Commander?

Who will be this generation's Jashobeam? Who will spurn the wisdom and the cautions of this world and stride out into battle against the 800? Who will be the first to gain the nickname from our anointed Shepherd?

Who will be this generation's Eleazar, this generation's Shammah? Who will cleave unto the hilt of the sword and not yield the ground purchased by the blood of our Christ? Who will spend themselves for the little parcels of barley and beans? Who will stand and fight when everyone else runs?

Who will be this generation's Benaiah? Who will prove the purest loyalty of heart and give themselves to the preservation of their King's body's health? Who will be fearless against the giants of sin and darkness? Who is willing to jump down into the pit, destroy the lion, and prove the overwhelming power of our God?

Who will be this generation's Abishai? Who has the guts to answer their King's outrageous request and say, "Yes, I will go with You! I will follow the Lamb whithersoever He goeth!"

Who will be chief among the captains in our generation? Who will be numbered amongst the mightiest? Who will be counted amongst the 37? Who will be named amongst the multitude, and who will be cherished as one of the few?

Please, don't overthink the situation. Don't ponder the dangers of such a seemingly reckless venture. Just go! Leave it all behind! Don't consult your flesh, for I can tell you ahead of time what it will say. It will scream for you to be careful. But the Mighties are not careful, cautious men—they are renegades with the mark of death upon them. The Mighties are supernatural demonstrations of courage, miracle men made powerful by their King. Sure they may die young, but they live life large with the stamp of heroic love tattooed upon their hearts, their foreheads, and their right thighs.

Believers like this are rare. But it is my great passion that such a version of Christianity will surface in this world once again.

I pray that you will step forward. And I pray that we can one day meet again and look back on this conversation as the moment when a mighty hero of God was born.

# *a moment for prayer*
## FINAL WORDS

### ⊰ LESLIE ⊱

Rather than trying to finish such a grand-themed book in my own paltry words, I have decided to let a great hero of prayer have the final say:

> The potency of prayer hath subdued the strength of fire; it hath bridled the rage of lions, hushed the anarchy to rest, extinguished wars, appeased the elements, expelled demons, burst the chains of death, expanded the gates of heaven, assuaged diseases, repelled frauds, rescued cities from destruction, stayed the sun in its course, and arrested the progress of the thunderbolt. Prayer is an all-sufficient panoply, a treasure undiminished, a mine which is never exhausted, a sky unobscured by clouds, a heaven unruffled by the storm. It is the root, the fountain, the mother, of a thousand blessings.
>
> —CHRYSOSTOM

# Notes

## Chapter 1—A Generation of Legendary Heroes

1. We recognize there is much confusion and debate among today's believers in regard to God's role versus Satan's role in tragedy and pain. For a more complete message on what Leslie and I believe in this specific area, visit discipleship.setapartlife.com and download a free copy of our message entitled "Fortification" under Eric's Discipleship series.

## Chapter 2—The Plague of Giants: a moment for prayer

1. Edith Deen, *Great Women of the Christian Faith* (Westwood, NJ: Barbour, 1959), 250.
2. C.H. Spurgeon, *The Metropolitan Tabernacle Pulpit* (London: Passmore & Alabaster, 1886), 116.

## Chapter 3—The Corrupted Throne

1. 1 Samuel 9:3.
2. Exodus 17:16.
3. Matthew 21:13; Mark 11:17; Luke 19:46.

## Chapter 3— The Corrupted Throne : a moment for prayer

1. Ian Thomas, *The Mystery of Godliness* (Grand Rapids: Zondervan, 1964), 162.

## Chapter 4—The Renegade Anointing: a moment for prayer

1. 1 Samuel 17:48.
2. Corrie ten Boom, *Tramp for the Lord* (Fort Washington, PA: Christian Literature Crusade, 2008), 170.
3. Horatio G. Spafford, "It Is Well with My Soul," written c. 1873.

## Chapter 5—The Season of Caves: a moment for prayer

1. E.M. Bounds, as cited in Leonard Ravenhill, *When Revival Tarries* (Minneapolis, MN: Bethany House, 1987), 24.
2. E.M. Bounds, *The Complete Works of E.M. Bounds on Prayer* (Grand Rapids: Baker, 1990), 23.

## Chapter 6—The Rush on Jebus

1. I should say it this way: There are certain aspects of Joab that I really desire to emulate. Joab is a mixed bag. He was quite an extraordinary warrior under David, but even with all his grit and gusto, he was a man who proved susceptible to his flesh.

## Chapter 6— The Rush on Jebus: a moment for prayer

1. Ian Thomas, *The Mystery of Godliness* (Grand Rapids: Zondervan, 1964), 185.
2. A.W. Tozer, *Divine Conquest* (Wheaton, IL: Tyndale House, 1995), 7.
3. Leslie Ludy, *Set-Apart Femininity* (Eugene, OR: Harvest House Publishers, 2008), 77-78.

## Chapter 7—The Company of Heroes

1. James 1:17; Hebrews 13:8.
2. 2 Samuel 2:18 NKJV.
3. 2 Samuel 21:19.
4. 2 Samuel 21:20-21.
5. In 1 Chronicles 11:10-47, an additional 16 mighty men are named in the list (verses 14-47).

## Chapter 7— The Company of Heroes: a moment for prayer

1. Leonard Ravenhill, *When Revival Tarries* (Minneapolis, MN: Bethany House, 1987), 153.
2. Ravenhill, *When Revival Tarries*, 87.
3. Ravenhill, *When Revival Tarries*, 108.

## Chapter 8—The 800 Dead: a moment for prayer

1. Matthew 6:25-34 (paraphrased).

## Chapter 9—The Pasdammim Parcel

1. 2 Corinthians 4:4,16.
2. 1 Thessalonians 5:17.
3. Luke 18:1.
4. 2 Corinthians 4:1.
5. Galatians 6:9; see also 2 Thessalonians 3:13.
6. Philippians 4:9.

## Chapter 9— The Pasdammim Parcel: a moment for prayer

1. Leonard Ravenhill, *When Revival Tarries* (Minneapolis, MN: Bethany House, 1987), 20.
2. Ravenhill, *When Revival Tarries*, 137.
3. E.M. Bounds, *The Complete Works of E.M. Bounds on Prayer* (Grand Rapids: Baker, 1990), 41-42.

## Chapter 10—The Snowy Pit: a moment for prayer

1. Andrew Bonar, as cited in Ravenhill, *When Revival Tarries*, 130.

## Chapter 11—While the Enemy Sleeps

1. This statement was recorded in the context of David conquering the seven hostile nations that still had a foothold in the Promised Land when David took the throne of united Israel.

## Chapter 11— While the Enemy Sleeps: a moment for prayer

1. Corrie ten Boom, *Tramp for the Lord* (Fort Washington, PA: Christian Literature Crusade, 2008), 145-47.
2. Ten Boom, *Tramp for the Lord*, 79-82.

## Chapter 12—The Cave of Adullum: a moment for prayer

1. Leonard Ravenhill, *When Revival Tarries* (Minneapolis, MN: Bethany House, 1987), 85.
2. Amy Carmichael, *Gold Cord* (London: Society for Promoting Christian Knowledge, 1947), 58.

*Wondering where to go from here?*
*take the next step...*

The Truth Is Worth Fighting For

# THE BRAVEHEARTED GOSPEL

ERIC LUDY

The battle of the ages is about to begin.

Death and life hang in the balance for millions.

You can make a difference.

The Bravehearted Gospel will show you how.

## A note from Eric and Leslie:

Throughout the centuries the true church of Jesus Christ has emerged out of war, culture, persecution, religion, apostasy and error. Today the true Church is emerging once again. Out of the ashes of dead religion, a struggle has been born between truth and deception that will alter the Church forever. By God's grace we intend to do everything in our power to see that living, vibrant and relevant historic Christianity rise from this conflict as the emergent victor to represent Jesus Christ for the next century and beyond with passion, love, honor and power. We invite you to join us - not in a conversation, not in a dialogue or a movement, but as a soldier of Jesus Christ in the battle of the ages. You can help change the world...

*Maybe one last time*